Harold B. Johnson

Sebastian
King of Portugal

Four Essays

Sebastian King of Portugal: Four Essays

Published by Wheatmark®
1760 East River Road, Suite 145
Tucson, Arizona 85718 U.S.A.
www.wheatmark.com

ISBN: 978-1-60494-998-8
LCCN: 2013937283

This little book is for
Valdemar Saagua Oliveira
friend and confidant

Table of Contents

By Way of
Introduction

My interest in King Sebastian was gradual and unfolding in nature, not something that happened all at once. It began, in fact, with my interest in Portugal's Prince Henry, "the Navigator"—the father, as it were, of European world imperialism. I read with admiration and pleasure the superb biography of Prince Henry written by the great British historian of Iberia, Sir Peter Russell. There, Sir Peter discusses the horoscope that was cast for Henry soon after his birth. In a footnote to this discussion, he indicates that the Biblioteca Nacional of Lisbon also houses some other unpublished horoscopes of Portuguese historical figures.

Sensing an opportunity to find a topic for a short article, I promptly went to the National Library and took a look at the documents for which he had given references. One of them, a *nacimento*—or birth chart—was of particular interest since it concerned King Sebastian of Portugal no less and had never been studied or published. I promptly went to work on it and produced an article that transcribed the horoscope with an accompanying commentary and analysis.[1] This article, now

---

1   First published in Harold Johnson, *Camponeses e Colonizadores* (Lisbon, 1997), 143–167.

1

published in English for the first time, is the opening essay in the present book.

In the course of studying the horoscope, I was led to Ptolemy's *Tetrabiblos* as the interpretive guide the author used to draw it up. Indeed, it soon became clear that this was where the writer of the horoscope got most of his ideas. However, the identity of the person who wrote the horoscope puzzled me for a time; I thought at first that the "Maldonado" who claimed to be the writer might possibly have been a theologian of the age. But quite soon afterward I discovered that "Maldonado" was one of the physicians whom Sebastian's mother, Joana de Austria, had brought with her from Castile when she went to Portugal to marry Sebastian's father. He was undoubtedly in attendance at Sebastian's birth and soon thereafter drew up his horoscope.[2]

Upon reading the horoscope, I was struck immediately by the inaccuracy of its predictions about Sebastian's future life. While perhaps 50 percent of its predictions were valid, the rest were dead wrong. This was particularly true with regard to Sebastian's family and sexual life. Instead of being "much given" to women, soon married, and the father of numerous progeny as predicted by his horoscope, Sebastian turned out to be allergic to women, never married, and was unable or unwilling to produce any offspring—one of the prime duties of royalty at the time. Probing deeper into the reason for all this became my consuming interest.

I immediately consulted the classic—and still unsurpassed—biography of Sebastian, that of Queiroz Velloso,[3] as well as a number of other biographies and works about him. After reading though all of these, what soon took shape for me was a kind of history of the history of Sebastian from around 1930 to the present. It became clear that his first defini-

---

2 As I point out in my article, it was common at the time for physicians to draw up horoscopes.

3 Queiroz Velloso, *D. Sebastiao*, 3rd ed., (Lisbon, 1945).

tive biography, by Velloso, came the closest to the objective truth about him. Significantly, this study was published in 1935, the same year in which Antonio Salazar had managed to put together the main elements of his reactionary/fascist New State. From then on, the study of Sebastian in Portugal was done under the watchful eye—and in the service of the ideology—of the New State. Thus the impartial objectivity of Queiroz Velloso was progressively replaced by the reactionary/fascist interpretation of Sebastian that still prevails to this day.

One of the aims of the reactionary/fascist interpretation was to "spin" the information about his infection with a sexually transmitted disease (STD), honestly and clearly treated by Velloso, to make sure that the issue became so muddy that no definite conclusion could be drawn. In a conscious betrayal of the search for the truth that should define historiography, what had been clear in Velloso—that Sebastian had contracted gonorrhea—became a famous "mystery illness." It was this denial of the truth that prompted me to dig deeper into the "nitty gritty" details about Sebastian's life. This I did in my essay entitled "A Pedophile in the Palace."[4] In the process I thought it important to identify his infector. Logic dictated that this would have to have been someone who had repeated access to him when he was nine—the age when his illness first became known—and who could have spent time with him alone without any chance of interruption from the outside. Clearly, in the mid-sixteenth century, the most likely person would have been his confessor. Indeed it is now well known, due to a profusion of inquisition documentation, that confessors often had sexual relations with their penitents. Everything in the practice of confession conspired to encourage this. The subject matter under discussion was often sexual "sin," and a confession could last a good long

---

4   Harold Johnson, *Dois Estudos Polémicos* (Tucson, 2004).

time. In addition, in the mid-sixteenth century, confessions brought the penitent and the confessor into intimate proximity.[5] Indeed, it was at about the time of Sebastian that Ignatius Loyola, father of the Jesuit Order and of Jesuit confession, was keen to "clean up" the situation by insisting that the penitent kneel *alongside* the confessor and not in front of him. In spite of these attempts at reform, inquisition records of the time are full of charges of sexual abuse in the confessional.

Somewhat later on, when I learned that Maria Augusta Lima Cruz, an historian at the University of the Minho, was about to write the most extensive biography of Sebastian since Queiroz Velloso, I took the liberty of sending her a draft copy of the article I was in the process of writing. She wrote back saying she found my ideas new and interesting and that they would be helpful to her in writing Sebastian's biography. Somewhat later I followed up by sending her a copy of the small book I wrote, in Portuguese, that included not only the pedophile essay but also a letter regarding Sebastian and his illness that I had exchanged with a prestigious professor of history at the University of Coimbra.[6] I had sent him a copy of my pedophile study, and he had replied with a somewhat condescending letter implying that I had let my imagination run away with me. This prompted from me a return letter in which I defended my thesis in no uncertain terms. After sending Lima Cruz my little book, all contact with her ceased. I could only suspect then, as I do now, that my frank defense of my thesis—described by a Brazilian colleague as "bruising and devastating" *(contundente e devastadora)* to

---

5   Henry Charles Lea, *A History of the Inquisition of Spain* (Macmillan, 1907), 96. The stall or confessional that separated penitent from confessor was a later development, with the precise purpose of keeping the penitent from physical proximity to the confessor. It was not made mandatory until 1614, and even then there was considerable resistance.

6   Harold Johnson, *Dois Estudos Polémicos* (Tucson, 2004).

the Coimbra historian—worried her about the professional danger to her career were she to get "into bed," so to speak, with my ideas. So when her biography[7] appeared, I found that, far from adopting any of my ideas, she spent some five-and-a-half pages in a disorganized and meandering attempt to refute them. I found her critique entirely unconvincing and said so in a review essay that I later published regarding her book—the third essay in this collection. Meanwhile, several reviews of my study that came out in the United States praised my work and accepted its validity. But when I attempted to publish my critical review of Cruz's biography in an online journal, five Portuguese historians who reviewed it refused to publish it.[8] In contrast, the *Portuguese Studies Review* in Canada was happy to publish it.

Thus it is clear that my research on and presentation of Sebastian are not much appreciated in Portugal. The best explanation for this is the fact that Sebastian, as I paint him, rubs badly against various Portuguese attitudes—especially the widespread homophobia there. But I have no doubt at all that I am much closer to the real person for the simple reason that I can approach the facts of his life without the encumbrance of Portuguese traditions and ideas about him. Coming from a society where homosexuality is much more accepted and acknowledged, and where there is far less homophobia, I can see him far more objectively and honestly.

In fact, probably only a non-Portuguese could achieve the objectivity necessary to see Sebastian as he truly was. During the centuries he spent as an icon coated over with all the unconscious as well as conscious national wishes that were projected onto him, barely any humanity remained. Certainly no sexuality was left to him; that had been wiped out entirely. And the culmination of that idolization and mystification

---

7   Maria Augusta Lima Cruz, *D. Sebastião* (Lisbon, 2009).
8   Onésimo Teotónio Almeida, José Luis Cardoso, Malfada Soares de Cunha, Luis Adão da Fonseca, and António Costa Pinto.

reached its acme in the controversy between Malheiro Dias and António Sérgio.[9] In the midst of all this, a note of simple good sense came from a very conservative Portuguese historian, Joaquim Veríssimo Serrão, who opined that "someday" Sebastian might be understood if approached from a psychological viewpoint. Of course Serrão was not the person to do so, since clearly his acquaintance with psychology was minimal—to say the least. But he was right in understanding the approach that would be needed, and the approach I use in my study.

There the matter rested until a few years ago a little book entitled *Retratos Ignorados de D. Sebastião* was published by a professor of labor law at the Catholic University of Lisbon.[10]

9   Maria Mota, "Sob o Signo de Prometeu: A polémica Sebastianista entre António Sérgio e Carlos Malheiro Dias (1924–1925)," to be found on the Internet at http://conferencias.ulusofona.pt/index.php/ lusocom/8lusocom09/paper/viewFile/162/138. Here is a part of the article: "Para Malheiro Dias, na linha da geração de 90, ser português significava manter-se fiel ao património cultural tradicional. Para a ideologia nacionalista que enformava esta geração, ofendida nos seus brios nacionais pelo Ultimato, D. Sebastião era um herói nacional, como se pode verificar em muitos dos textos literários da época e, muito em especial no poema "O Desejado" de António Nobre, que exerceu enorme influência na poesia portuguesa deste período.Politicamente, Carlos Malheiro Dias era um defensor do integralismo lusitano: a visão do mundo que enformava a sua defesa do culto sebástico era tradicionalista, monárquica e católica. António Sérgio, pelo contrário, era um espírito cosmopolita e democrata. Patriota, o seu patriotismo nunca se confundiu com o dogmatismo nacionalista, professado pelos monárquicos conservadores. Muito pelo contrário, a cidadania nacional fazia parte da sua representação como cidadão do mundo. Não por acaso era um "estrangeirado" termo que adjectiva aqueles que como ele defendiam a re-integração de Portugal no âmbito cultural europeu, o que exigia, na sua opinião, uma radical reforma das mentalidades, ou seja, a passagem de uma mentalidade dogmática e acrítica para uma mentalidade crítica e científica. Discordando da concepção patrimonial e memorialística dos defensores do tradicionalismo, as "pedras vivas" eram para ele, verdadeiramente, a Pátria, os homens vivos do presente e não o património herdado" (2127–2128).

10   Bernardo da Gama Lobo Xavier, *Retratos Ignorados de D. Sebastião* (Estoril, 2008).

When this came to my attention, I had no idea what the book contained, other than that it involved some paintings of Sebastian that I wanted to see.

But when I got a copy of the book, I was both astonished and delighted to find that, perhaps without realizing it, the author had provided the final confirmation and proof of my thesis.[11] This is what I explain in the last review/essay in my little book.

Harold B. Johnson

---

11   I might note here that the author, Lobo Xavier, is careful never to mention my essay on Sebastian—although he had to be aware of it since it is discussed at some length by Cruz in the biography that he claims to have read with much care. Thus it is likely that when he refers to the "moral assassination" of Sebastian he is thinking of my study. Since I make it clear that I don't regard Sebastian's being abused sexually at age nine nor his subsequent development as a homosexual as due to any "moral" fault of his, but simply as facts resulting from bad luck given his circumstances, Lobo Xavier's outdated idea that homosexuality is somehow "wicked," an attitude that most modern mentalities have overcome, is clearly in evidence.

A Horoscope Cast Upon the Birth of King Sebastian of Portugal (1554–1578)

A generous reference in Peter Russell's recent biography of Prince Henry, "the Navigator"[1] led me recently to the manuscript of a "nativity" or natal horoscope cast for the future King Sebastian soon after his birth in 1554.[2]

As Russell makes clear, great store was set by horoscopes at royal courts during the Renaissance and early modern periods, and Portugal certainly was no exception to this.[3]

---

1   Peter Russell, *Prince Henry the Navigator: A Life* (New Haven, 2000), 375. Russell discusses historical horoscopes in general and that of Prince Henry in particular on pages 15–159.

2   Biblioteca Nacional de Lisboa (BNL), *Reservados*, COD 8920, ff. 39v–41v. My transcription of the document is given in Appendix I.

3   For example, on July 9, 1493, D. João II made a gift of ten gold "espadins" to Rabi Abraão, "estrolico." On late medieval and Renaissance astrology see S. J. Tester, *A History of Western Astrology* (Woodbridge: Suffolk, 1987); Maxime Préaud, *Les Astrologues à Fin du Moyen Age* (Paris, 1984); Hilary M. Carey, *Courting Disaster: Astrology at the English Court and University in the Later Middle Ages* (London, 1992); Eugenio Garin, *Astrology in the Renaissance: the Zodiac of Life* (London, 1983); Robert K. DeKosky, *Knowledge and Cosmos: Development and Decline of the Medieval Perspective* (Washington, 1979); *Dicionário de*

Indeed, King Manuel, "the Fortunate," the great-grandfather

História de Portugal, *s.v.* "Astrología." Astrology was generally divided into two parts: so-called "natural astrology" that concerned itself with the weather—when it might rain or snow, or when droughts might occur, as well as matters of illness and health—and "judiciary astrology," which attempted to predict the course of one's life or one's character from the conjunction of the planets at the time of one's birth. The first was considered generally licit although often erroneous. On the other hand, "judiciary" astrology was "totally superstitious" and forbidden by the Roman Church because it was thought to infringe upon the doctrine of free will: see Juan Machado de Chaves, *Perfeto Confessor y Cura de Almas* (Madrid, 1647), I, 241; and the bull of Sixtus V of 1586, *Terrae et Coeli Creator*, that I have edited and freely translated in Appendix III from the Latin text in *Bullarium Privilegiorum ac Diplomatum Romanorum Pontificum Amplissima Collectio*, tomus quartus, pars quarta, ab anno X. GREGORII XIII usque ad annum III. SIXTI V, scilicet ab anno 1581 ad 1588 (Rome, 1747), 176–179. In addition to the Roman Church, there were also other critics of judicial astrology—especially after the publication of Giovanni Pico della Mirandola's *Disputationes adversus astrologiam divinatricem* in 1497 (see the edition of Eugenia Garin [Florence, 1952]). For the reign of João III, see Christóvão Rodrigues Acenheiro, "Chroncias dos Senhores Reis de Portugal," *Collecção de Inéditos de História Portuguesa* (Lisbon, 1936), V, 363: "Nom deixo d'escrever que hu Estroleguo saiba a vertude dos Planetas máas, ou boas de suas influemcias pro suas regras Astrologais naturalmente: o Senhor Deos he sobre natural, e ussa de sua piadade como o que fês milagrosamente: Deos aterno, que todo vê amte sim, e Estroleguo vê por pineiras, como sol cris; e asim que fica emguanado com seu saber, como se vê cada dia ao olho." In 1523, Fr. António de Beja, a Portuguese follower of Pico della Mirandola, also wrote—interestingly enough at the request of Dona Leonor, possiblly the widow of King Manuel—a tract inveighing against judicial astrology, *Contra os Juízos dos Astrólogos* (1523): see the edition of J. de Pina Martins, *Fr. António de Beja contra a Astrologia Judicíaria* (Lisbon, 1962). Luis de Albuquerque is the author of some interesting comments about criticism of the astrological arts in Portugal during the sixteenth century: *Crónicas de História de Portugal* (Lisbon, 1987), 107–111.

of Sebastian, was well known for his devotion to astrology and astrological science.[4] It therefore comes as no surprise that he saw to it that his son, the future João III, was taught, along with his Virgil and Sallust, the rudiments of astrology from a tender age. According to Francisco de Andrade, João, along with some other children of the court, was tutored by D. Diogo Ortiz de Vilhegas, bishop of Tanger, who "read him … the counsels of Cato, read him Terence, Virgil, Sallust and some part(s) of the Bible; the theory of the planets and some easy things about astrology he heard from Tomás de Torres, an eminent doctor and astrologer of that time."[5]

Later in the 1550s, Cipião de Aragão, a Neapolitan-born

---

4   Damião de Góis, *Crónica do Felicíssimo Rei D. Manuel* (Coimbra, 1955), 21–202. King Manuel (1495–1521) set high store by his doctor, Tomás de Tôrres, a "homem mui experto, assi na Astrologia, quomo em outras sciencias," and is reported to have consulted him regarding the stars and the planets before deciding when to send his ships to India. He also favored other astrologers such as a certain "Mestre João" to whom he granted a *tença* of 12$000 *reais* on January 1, 1514 (Anselmo Braamcamp Freire, *Crítica e Historia* vol I [Lisbon,1910], 249).

5   Francisco de Andrada, *Chrónica de D. João III*, ed. M. Lopes de Almeida (Porto: 1976), 6: "leolhe … os conselhos de Catão, leolhe Terencio, Virgílio, Salustio, e alguma parte da Bíblia: a teorica dos planetas, e algumas cousas faciles da astrologia ouuio de Tomas de torres medico e austrologo naquelle tempo insigne." Torres was most likely the doctor [physician] satirized by Gil Vicente in his *Auto dos Físicos*:

"Bisexto he anno agora,
em Picis estava Jupiter,
Saturno ha de desfazer
quanto natureza melhora:
bem ha qui que guarecer.
Tambem em Picis a luna …
isso foy em quarta feyra;
Mercurio à ora primeyra …
nam vejo causa nenhuma
pera febre verdadeyra."

astrologer then much in vogue in Portugal, received various astrological commissions including one to predict whether or not the illness of Sebastian's father was going to prove fatal.[6] (It was.)

So far, however, no one aside from Russell appears to have noticed this particular horoscope, cast soon after the birth of Sebastian by Fernão Abarca Maldonado, one of the medical doctors whom Dona Juana brought with her from Castile.[7] It is remarkably full and holds for us, I think, a special interest given his ultimate destiny as King.

The horoscope begins by choosing the Ascendant, or

See Anselmo Braamcamp Freire, *Gil Vicente Trovador, Mestre da Balança*, (Lisbon: 1944), 96–97.

6   *Auctos de Cipião dAragona napolitano morador en esta cydade de Lixboa preso no carcere do Sancto officio* apud Francisco Bethencourt, "Astrologia e Sociedade no Século XVI: Uma primeira abordagem," *Revista de História Economica e Social*, VIII (Lisbon: Sa da Costa, 1981), 68–71.

7   When I published an earlier version of this study in my *Campone-ses e Colonizadores* (Lisbon: Estampa, 2002), I could only specu-late about the identity of the Maldonado. Now I can be certain that it was cast, without doubt, by Dr. Fernan (or Fernando or Fernão) Abarca Maldonado, a *médico* from an important Sala-mancan family who came to Portugal in the entourage of Sebas-tian's mother, Doña Juana de Áustria. See José Maria de Queiroz Velloso, *D. Sebastião, 1554–1578,3rd. ed.*, (Lisbon, 1935), 14. As was so often the case at the time, *physicos* or medical doctors were also versed in astrology and cast horoscopes as part of their profession. Dr. Maldonado was likely in attendance when Sebas-tian was born and thus would have had a very exact knowledge of the time of his birth. Also Sousa Viterbo, *Notícia sobre Alguns Médicos Portuguezes* (Lisbon, 1895), 46–47. On February 12, 1554—shortly after Sebastian's birth— King João III provided Maldonado with a *tença vitalícia* of 40$000 per year for services rendered to Doña Juana (*minha filha*), as well as for those expected from him in the future. Maldonado died in Portugal in October of 1574.

First House, of Sebastian's chart as the "principal predictor" of his life. The existence of three planets (the Sun, Mars, and Mercury) in the twelfth house of the horoscope, with the Sun opposite its own house (Leo)—see chart—indicates that Sebastian's early years will be "difficult." Still, because of the location of Venus and Jupiter, the benefic planets, and their relationship to Saturn, it will be possible for him to survive the problems that arise during his childhood.

Mercury in the twelfth house, and the Moon in the sixth, will cause Sebastian to be persistent in pursuing his aims and give him good judgment. Mercury is also under the rule of Saturn, which will give him good understanding and wisdom. On the other hand, the malefic planet, Saturn, is located in the Ascendant or first house and will make him deceitful at times and inclined to go back on his word.

Venus in "sextile aspect" (a favorable position) to the Ascendant promises him a good memory, patience, and love of letters. In addition, the situation of Venus indicates that he will be much given to "pleasures" with women—and musical instruments—as well as to clothes, song, scents, and horses. In general, because of the "temper" of his body, he will sometimes prove to be extremely gay and at other times very melancholic.

This temper will be cold and humid, or "phlegmatic," as is indicated by the Ascendant and sextile rays of Venus. Furthermore, in appearance he will be dark (*preto*) and short, but nonetheless elegant and attractive due to the aforesaid sextile rays of Venus and to Saturn's location in the house of Jupiter. Saturn in that house gives him some facial deformity, but the influence of Venus lessens it.

Illnesses will come to him because the Moon is in the sixth house and its rays, hostile to Mercury, indicate a loose complexion and illness in the parts of the body signified by Leo—namely the heart, back, or stomach. The Moon in the sixth house also indicates that he will have weak eyes, while the position of Saturn will bring him pains in the right ear and in the bladder. All this will happen to him in his early years.

The Sun in his chart is accompanied by three great *infortunios* (malefic planets); this indicates that his father either is dead or will die shortly, unless the goodness of the Lord does not intervene.[8] The Moon in the middle of the heart of Leo indicates that Sebastian will have great authority and powers of command. Saturn in the first house indicates either that he is the first-born, or that all of his siblings have died.

The nobility will be much "dearer" to him than the "people" (*povo*) because of Jupiter's position as lord of the Ascendant. And because of the opposition of Mercury and the Moon—see chart—he will be confronted by some acts of sedition by the common people. Venus in the eleventh house will fill him with confidence, while the Moon in the eastern quarter of his chart indicates that he will be married in his youth to a good and virtuous wife who will give him children, all of whom will be noble, handsome, and fortunate. Venus in the sign of Capricorn will stimulate his sexuality, but this will take place within the context of his marriage.

With regard to his choice of residence, he will find Lisbon to be suitable since it is under the sign of Libra, "where Jupiter is found." Other favorable locations are those under the signs of Pisces and Sagittarius, as well as those under Jupiter and Venus. Unsuitable places for him are those that are beneath the lords of the signs of the sixth, eighth, and twelfth houses of Saturn and Mars.

---

8   One has to suspect here that Maldonado had some knowledge, independent of the horoscope, that Sebastian's father had died shortly before his birth. In addition, the provision that God could reverse the fate decreed by the stars would appear to be a concession to those critics of judicial astrology who condemned it on the grounds that it usurps the powers of God.

Now let us attempt to assess as far as possible the accuracy of the predictions made in his horoscope by comparing them with the relevant facts as known.

1. He would have difficult (*dificil i trabalhosa*) childhood.

Sebastian had Aleixo de Menenses as his guardian (*aio*) from the age of four up to his fourteenth year (1568), when he assumed the throne in his own right. He also had the services of a tutor, the Jesuit Luís Gonçalves da Câmara.[9] Sebastian turned out to be a child difficult to deal with and somewhat unbalanced in spite of having a lively intelligence ("de difícil trato e com um certo desequilíbrio psicológico, apesar de possuidor de uma inteligência viva.")[10] Taught reading by his *aio* and humane letters by his tutor, Sebastian was considered a good, indeed quite bright, pupil. However, the knowledge he acquired—while varied—revealed according to Velloso, "uma estranha confusão de ideias [and] uma obscuridade de pensamento."[11] In spite of this, Sebastian is described as proud (*orgulhoso*) and unruly, holding a high opinion of himself and increasingly resentful of the discipline to which his paternal grandmother, dowager Queen Catherine, subjected him.[12] The overall result of the education that he received from Câmara was to turn him into a *beato*,[13]

---

9   Câmara, for whom Sebastian would appear to have developed a genuine affection, was anything but attractive: he stuttered and was blind in one eye.

10   J. J. Alves Dias, *Portugal do Renascimento à Crise Dinástica* (Lisbon, 1998), 746.

11   J. M. Queirós Velloso, "História Política" in *História de Portugal*, V (Barcelos, 1933) 49.

12   Since she apparently forced Sebastian to sleep in the same room as she did up to the age of seven, his resentment of her may well have had some cause: Ibid., 50.

13   The male equivalent of *beata*: "Homen dado a rezar, e a devoções com descuido dos seus deveres" (*Diccionario da Lingua Portu-*

although he also developed an intense liking for horseback riding, jousting, and hunting.

2. His horoscope predicted that he would be "constant and firm" in the things he proposed to do and would further have a good sense of justice, excellent understanding, and the capacity to give good advice.

Sebastian was regarded as rather more than merely "constant and firm" in what he proposed to do; in certain matters, he was clearly "obsessed." Paramount among these was his determination to lead an ill-conceived "crusade" against the Moors in Morocco—a goal that he pursued so obstinately, and against all wiser advice, that he became the despair of sensible minds at court. He managed, however, to ignore and overcome all sage counsel and ended up leading his army to destruction in the battle of Alcazer-Kebir.[14] Hence, while the horoscope is right about his "firmness and constancy," it is completely wrong with regard to his *boom entendimento e excellente conselho*.

3. Sebastian was predicted to be pertinacious in "avarice" and endowed with a "very big heart" that would lead him

gueza, s.v. "Beata.") Indeed, Sebastian was noted for going to confession every eight days, something apparently considered remarkable in court circles of the time.

14   According to Velloso, Sebastian prayed to God to make him into His captain for war against the infidel: "Era uma ideia fixa que se foi pouco a pouco transformando na orgulhosa convicção de estar predestinado para grandes cousas" (52); also, "A brandura e letras que auia de misturar com a altiuez de seu espirito por estranha metamerfose se conuertia em brios affeição à guerra que com as primeiras palauras hia concebendo as materias que auia de treladar e omitido as lições que auia de ouuir tudo erão estimulos de intempestiua e desproporcionada gloria": in Luciano Ribeiro, "Documentos Inéditos para a História do Reinado de D. Sebastião," *Stúdia*, V (1960), 38.

to attempt great and elevated undertakings (*grandes i altas empresas*) described as a good thing for princes and "especially for their poor."

As far as any signs of avarice, Sebastian was reputed to show none whatsoever; rather, it is his "liberality" that is remembered.[15] With regard to attempts at "great and elevated undertakings," this is surely how he would have viewed his determination to lead a crusading army into Morocco. Finally, in spite of the horoscope's prediction that the nobility would be "dearer" to him than the "povo," his legislation is generally regarded as having done a good deal to protect the interests of the "less fortunate" of his subjects.[16]

4. He was predicted to have a "good memory," as well as patience and a love of letters.

Although he was regarded as a bright and apt pupil, he was most definitely not noted for his patience, but rather for his quasi-pathological impetuousness; as far as his other interests went, while he fancied himself something of an

---

15   Joaquim V. Serrão, "Documentos Inéditos para a História do reinado de D. Sebastião," *Boletim da Biblioteca da Universidade de Coimbra*, XXIV (1958), 123: "Foy elRey D. Sebastião de condiçaõ muy liberal, sem mostra alguma de cobiça."

16   Francisco de Sales Loureiro, "D. Sebastião e Alcácer Quibir," in José H. Saraiva, dir., *Historia de Portugal*, IV (1983), 137: "A preocupação social empregna o sentido mais amplo na sua legislação-caso verdadeiramente único no século XVI. Muitas são as leis que revelam ser seu primacial objectivo evitar a opressão do povo, especialmente dos mais desfavorecidos." Whether this actually did much for the poor is doubtful since in fact income inequality was rising markedly in Portugal during his reign: see the relevant information in Harold B. Johnson, "Malthus Confirmed? Being Some Reflections on the Changing Distribution of Wealth and Income in Portugal (1309–1789)," (unpublished).

intellectual, most of his interest was directed toward military matters.

5. He would be much given to "pleasures" with women, musical instruments, clothing, songs, scents, and horses.

If there was anything which did *not* interest Sebastian, it was women,[17] and his open aversion to them was often noted and much commented on by his contemporaries. Whether he had much use for musical instruments, songs, or scents is not known. On the other hand, he did like to ride horseback and was devoted to jousting and hunting.

6. Since his chart placed Venus in the sign of Capricorn, Sebastian should have been given to all the things signified by Saturn and Venus. This would make him sometimes very gay, and at other times very melancholic, due to the cold and humid—that is to say phlegmatic— temper of his body. In appearance he should have been dark (*preto*) and of small stature, but nonetheless beautiful and elegant. He would also have some deformity in his face, but Venus would lessen, if not remove, this defect.

---

17   "Os padres do triumuirato [i.e., his aio, Meneses; his tutor, Câmara; and his confessor, Fr. Luiz de Montoya; or possibly instead, Câmara; Leão Henriques, the Jesuit confessor to Cardinal Henry; and Miguel de Torres, Jesuit confessor to Dowager Queen Catarina] dissimulauão acomodandose ao seu castissimo Rey, segundo a uoz comuna pelo menos inimigo publico de mulheres".: LR, Documentos, 50; also: "elRey de nenhuma maneira pode ver molher," Manuel Lopes de Almeida, ed., *Memorial de Pero Roiz Soares* (Coimbra, 1953) 44. See also the letter to Philip II's from one of his envoy-reporters at the Portuguese court, Don Juan da Silva: "elRey muestra tanto odio a las mujeres, que aparta los ojos dellas, e se una dama le sierve la copa, busca como tomarla sin tocarle la mano" quoted in Joaquim V. Serrão, *Historia de Portugal*, III (Lisbon, 1978), 69.

The personality of King Sebastian, according to one specialist on his reign, was *não equilibrada*, denoting a lack of good sense as well as an impulsive and capricious nature demanding obedience. His surviving letters reveal a confusion of ideas and repetition of narrative material that almost never responds to the questions supposedly addressed.[18]

His appearance as he grew up was certainly not that predicted by his horoscope. Instead of small or short, he was of medium height; he was not dark, but had reddish-blond hair and blue eyes set in a white face with freckles[19]. His lower lip was very full, giving him—in the portrait of 1571—a rather feminine, "rosebud" mouth.

7. Sebastian was predicted to fall sick because of his weakness and loose complexion. His heart, back, and stomach were supposed to be particularly vulnerable. He would also have weak eyesight and pains in his right ear, as well as problems with his hearing and his bladder. These things were to occur during his early years.

Sebastian's health problems began around the age of eleven, according to Velloso.[20] But they did not, so far as is known, involve his heart, back, or stomach. Rather, he suffered from a malady described as the "expulsion of a certain substance from his organs." Velloso has opined that this was some sort of seminal ejaculation or effusion, very possibly gonorrheal.[21] According to the sources, it was exac-

---

18   Joaquim V. Serrão, *Historia de Portugal*, III (Lisbon, 1978), 68.

19   His appearance at age seventeen is known to us from the oil portrait of him by Cristóvão de Morais (1571), now in the Museu Nacional de Arte Antiga (Lisbon), where he appears reasonably tall and with reddish-blond hair. There are no noticeable facial defects, and the artist, quite understandably, does not paint his freckles.

20   *Velloso*, 53.

21   Sebastian expelled "por sus organos cierta substancia" according

erbated by the violent exercise he often took on horseback or hunting, and receded when he was quiet. But along with these "effusions," he also suffered from attacks of vertigo and fainting spells. His ailments were the object of considerable international interest, especially to Philip II of Spain, who kept himself informed about them through special envoys that he placed in the Portuguese court. Because of these reports he remained hesitant about promising his eldest daughter, Isabel Clara Eugénia, to Sebastian in marriage.

8. The condition and life of persons born under the sign of Venus are better and happier than those of parents who are born under the sign of the sun when the sun carries with it three great misfortunes: either the father is dead; he will die before long; or he will experience some great misfortune "if the goodness of our Lord does not prevent it."

The horoscope is entirely correct here, which makes one wonder if its author might not have had special knowledge of his subject. Sebastian's father Prince João, the son of King João III, was sickly for most of his short life (1537–1554), suffering probably from juvenile diabetes.[22] He died on January 2, 1554, eighteen days before his only son was born.

9. Sebastian would become the leader of a band of young men whom he would support.

---

to Castilian reporters. I discuss this matter further in APPENDIX II.

22   João would have had "type I" diabetes, now thought to be caused by a viral infection or some nutritional factor in childhood or early adulthood [see *The Merck Manual of Medical Information* (Whitehouse Station, NJ, 1997), 718]. He suffered from abnormal thirst but was prohibited by his doctors from drinking enough water to quench it. He died on January 2, 1554, soon after he frantically downed a considerable amount of rainwater that he had managed, in desperation, to collect for himself.

It was arranged for Sebastian to have about him a small group of young noblemen with whom he studied his lessons; later on, he was accompanied by a group called his "chaco-tada," with whom he "joked around"—most likely with them as the butt of his jokes rather than the reverse. He was also rumored to spend his nights with "gente de pouca autoridade e menos mostras de uirtude."[23]

10. He would be married in his youth to a good and faithful wife who would give him noble and handsome children.

Sebastian's possible marriage partners were an ongoing matter of international diplomacy. He was tentatively linked to a number of candidates, but nothing ever came of it[24] due both to Sebastian's repeated procrastination regarding the matter—most probably the result of his undisguised dislike of feminine company—as well as to Philip II's hesitation in marrying any of his daughters to a man with a possible venereal disease and an unstable personality. Unmarried, and possibly homosexual, Sebastian obviously produced no children. The predictions of his horoscope go blatantly wrong here.

11. Lisbon, as well as places under the signs of Pisces, Sagit-tarius, Jupiter, and Venus would be appropriate places for him to live, while those beneath the lords of the signs of the sixth, eighth, and twelfth houses of Saturn and Mars would not.

---

23   LR, *Documentos*, 44.
24   On the various marriage negotiations that went on, see, inter alia, Joaquim V. Serrão, *Historia de Portugal*, III (Lisbon, 1978), 68–69; and the detailed account in Francisco Rodrigues, S. J., *História de Companhia de Jesus na Assistência de Portugal*, 2 vols., (Porto, 1938), II:2, 313–340.

Sebastian never traveled north of the Mondego river and seldom farther north than Santarém. He preferred the south—the Alentejo and the Algarve—and spent most of his time in four localities: Lisbon, Almerim, Sintra, and Evora.[25]

So, how well did Sebastian's "nativity" do in predicting the events of his life? The most that can be said, I think, is it that it got some things surprisingly right and others astonishingly wrong: not much better than simple chance. Among the former were its predictions about his "difficult" childhood, his determination to pursue his dreams, his efforts to help the common people, and the fact that he would suffer numerous ailments—although it failed to predict the exact nature of these correctly. It also proved correct with regard to his father's early demise and the fact that Sebastian would be the leader of a gang of young men.

On the other hand it went badly astray regarding his sexuality and marriage, predicting that he would be intensely interested in women, be married early on to a faithful wife and have many children. What in fact happened was almost exactly the opposite: his lack of interest in women was notorious; he avoided getting married; and he certainly had no children. The nativity was also very mistaken about his appearance. Instead of small and dark, he was of middling stature with blue eyes, reddish-blond hair, and freckles.

Whether or not he was aware of the horoscope, and—if so—whether it played any role in shaping his life's goals, is not known. There is little evidence that he made any particular effort to fulfill predictions, as Russell indicates that his

---

25   J. J. Alves Dias, op. cit., 746–747. Whether or not the places where he chose to reside were influenced to any degree by his horoscope, I cannot say; I have not been able to determine the astrological signs under which these towns [aside from Lisbon] are situated.

ancestor Prince Henry did in the case of his own horoscope.[26] But if in fact he ignored it, the main reason may well have been its very mistaken predictions about his appearance, something that would have been noticed early on. Indeed, this may well have led him and others to regard most of the rest of it as unworthy of much credence.

---

26   Russell, 18.

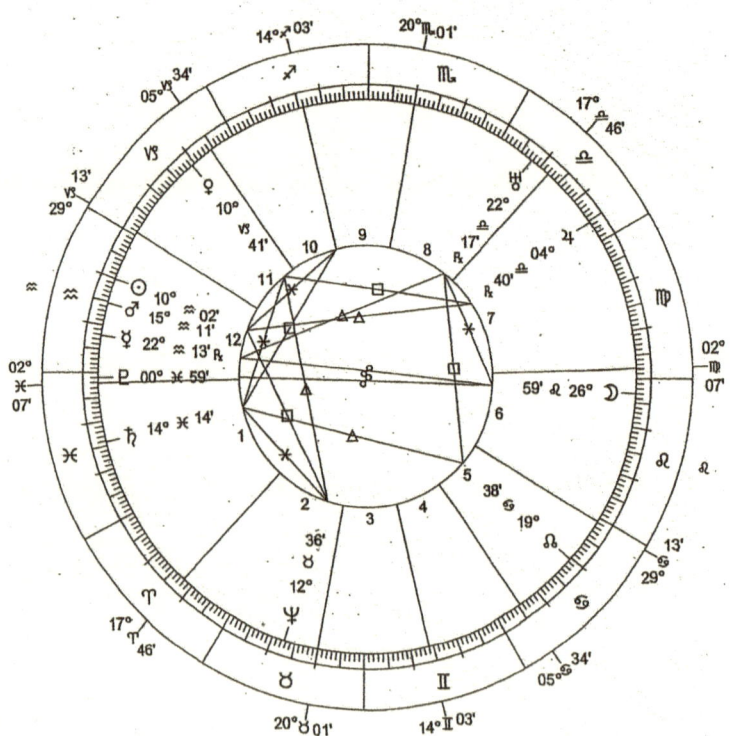

Natal Chart of Dom Sebastião
Lisbon, Portugal; 08:15 AM
January 20, 1554

Appendix I

Transcription of the Nacimento

(f. 39v.)

V nacimento del rei dom sebastiao noso/senhor
tirado pollo f maldonado.[27]

naõ achando neste nacimento dia nem ao sol/ nem a lluã
nem ao senhor da oposicaõ precedente/ a esta nacenca em
llugares proprios pera seu signi/ficador da uida, ho atribuo
ao ascendente o qual/ como principal significador de uida,
polla doutrina/ de tolopmeu[28] (sic), sera necesario dirigir ao
corpo i rraios/ malignos de planetas que contrariaõ a uida o
que/ se podera fazer em tempo i em llugar, pollo pre/semte he

---

27   The author of the horoscope was Fernão Abarco Maldonado,
one of the doctors who came to Portugal in the entourage of his
mother, Dona Juana de Austria. See footnote 7.

28   He doubtless refers to Claudius Ptolemy, the Alexandrine astronomer-geographer of the second century A.D. Maldonado's presentation and interpretation of the horoscope shows that he was
using Ptolemy's *Tetrabiblos* as a guide, and he follows it closely
throughout his commentary on the horoscope. See Ptolemy, *Tetrabiblos*, ed. and trans. By F. E. Robbins (Cambridge, 1998),
passim.[Hereafter "TB"]. It is unlikely, though possible, that
Maldonado used the Greek text (first printed by Froben at
Nurnberg in 1535); more likely he used a Latin translation (first
one printed in 1484).

necesaria uer da criaçaõ// (f.40r) A criaçaõ deste senhor sera dificil i trabalhosa porque tres planetas estaõ em a dozena casa i o sol huma dellas[29] estaa em a oposicaõ da sua/ casa conJunto com mars i a lluã em a sexta casa/ i o ascendemte com saturno; todavia estando uenus/quase a direito da planeta sobre o ascendente bem/ desposta i em fauorauel rresguardo daquelle ascendente/i de Jupiter seu senhor i mais o sol no trono de/ Jupiter i uenus lleuando os rraios deste Jupiter a/ Saturno; todos as quais cousas daõ tal socorro/ a uida deste naçido que podera pasar os anos de/ criacaõ[30] posto que aja a dificuldade que digo/

Mercurio i a lluã estando em signos fixos[31] i moui/mento tardo imcliaõ a uontade deste nacido a ser/ constante i firme nas cousas que propuser de fazer/ i lhe daõ segurança de justica i mais estando mer/curio na casa de saturno com algunas estrelas fixas/ de sua natura o fazem de boom emtendimento i exce/llente conselho; todauia esta significacaõ sera algumas/ uezes trocada a mal como sera emganar i tras/tocar o detre-miado; o que estaa confirmado por satur/no constituido do ascendente. o qual llugar eu inclino/ a emganar[32] i ser pertinaz em auaricia i doado de/ coracaõ muito grande com itento de grandes i altas/ empresas, cousa boa a principes i principalmente/ pera pobres. O aspeito sextil de uenus nas

29   Though Copernicus's work on the solar system was printed in 1543, it obviously had not been disseminated or accepted in Europe by 1554; hence the sun is still regarded as one of the planets that circle the earth, center of the universe.

30   TB, 253: For Ptolemy the first stage of life went from birth to age four; the second from four to fourteen.

31   The "fixed signs" of the Zodiac are Taurus, Leo, Scorpio and Aquarius.

32   The sense of this phrase is not entirely clear. It might be that Maldonado is commenting upon his own abilities; on the other hand, the sense might be that he is inclined to see the position of Saturn as indicative of Sebastian's deceitful nature.

par/tes interiores do ascendente daa graca aos comdi/cõs;
Saturno taõbem em aspeito fauorauel de ue/nus lhe doa boa
memoria, paciencia, delleitacaõ aas/ lletras i a toda rrezaõ;
que todo este prazer daa uenus/ (40v) estando bem desposta;
digo que este nacido sera muito dado a seus prazeres como a
molheres/ instrumentos musicais, uestidos, cantigas, cheiros/
i cauallos ho que he testemunho disto uenus estan/do no
signo do capricornio i asi sera inclinado/ i dado a todas as
cousas significados por/saturno i uenus donde aquecera/ que
algumas/ uezes sera eXtremamente allegre i muito ma/llon-
conico o que lhe procedera pollas tempernaça/ do corpo de
que agora fallarei.

A temperança do corpo sera frio i humedo que se chama/
fleimatico porque asi o testemunha o ascendente i os/ rraios
sextilles de uenus; este todauia parteçipara/ mais de secura
polla presemça de saturno no mesmo/ amgulo do ascend-
nete i a lluã em a seXta casa na/ oposiçaõ do aspeito de
mercurio, donde aquecera que/sera preto i de pequeno
corpo[33] i todauia fermosura/ i rraca por rrezaõ dos ditos
rraios seXtiles de uenus/ no ascendente i saturno que he
achado na casa de Jupi/ter; este saturno no dito llugar daa
alguma diffor/midade no rrosto mas o aspeito de uenus o tira
i/o deminuie.

As doenças lhe uiraõ porque a lluã estando na seXta casa/
omde caem os rraios opositos a mercurio mostraõ/ fraqueza
i copleiçaõ flaco i mal na parte do corpo/ que he significada
do signo do lliaõ a lluã he como/ seja o coracao o costado i o
estamago; ha significacaõ taobem de ter alguma flaqueza nos
olhos por rrezaõ/ que a lluã estaa na seXta casa na casa do
sol i o ascen/dente com a costolaçaõ i o sol com ascendente

---

33   TB, 309: "If Saturn is setting, in appearance he makes them
      dark, slender, small, straight-haired, with little hair on the body,
      rather graceful, and black-eyed."

do capricornio/(f.41r) Saturno daa door na orelha direita[34] i
no ouço i/ na bexiga as quais cousas lhe uirão na primeira/
idade/

O estado i uida de mais que he significado e aos nacenças/
ordiarias por uenus saõ muito milhores i ditosas que os/ dos
pais que saõ rrepresentadas pello sol, na nacenca este/ sol
estando ifortunado de tres grandes infortunios mostra/ o pai
ser morto ou que em breue morrera ou que caira/ em alguum
grande infortunio[35] se a bondade de noso senhor/ lhe naõ
socorre.

A lluã estando com huma estrella no meo do coraçaõ do liaõ/
promete muito grande autoridade i poder pera mandar/ o que
staa seguro por jupiter senhor do ascendente i da decima/
i saturno na primeira casa o mostra primeiro nascido/ por
natura ou por morte de seus irmaõs se os tiuese[36]/ A nobreza
lhe sera muito mais cara que o pouo porque jupiter/ he senhor
do ascendente i da coraçaõ do ceo donde aquecera que/ expri-
mentara algumas sedicois do pouo aa causa da oposiçaõ/ de
mercurio i da lluã. Venus na omzena casa o emche de/ con-
fianca i esperanca de poder auer tudo o que elle desejar i
mui/to grandes rriquezas em a quesicaõ das quais sera muito/
imtento porque Jupiter significador das rriquezas he rresguar/
do de uenus. A lluã em aquarta parte oriental diz que/ elle
sera casado em sua mocidade i sera sua molher boa/ i honesta
que he significada por jupiter em a septima/ casa[37] i venus
em trino aspeito da casa septima nota/ que sera a norrecedor

---

34   TB, 319: "Saturn is lord of the right ear."
35   TB, 245, discusses the signs governing the state of the father.
36   TB, 253: "In case Saturn is in the ascendant, they are the first-
      born or the first to be reared."
37   TB, 393: "For men [with regard to their marriage] it is necessary
      to observe the position of the moon in their genitures. For ... if
      she chances to be in the eastern quadrants she makes men
      marry young; ... if the planets to which she applies, either by

de companhia de mancebos, porque a lluã i/ uenus saõ lliu-
radas de corrupcaõ i aspeito de todos infortu/nios. Aimda que
venus no signo de capricornio lha daa/ inclinacaõ gramde nas
cousas uenereas. Aimda que esto sera/ com ligitimo matrimonio. o tempo do qual se achara pelas dirreições i as emcerra
uenus i na omzena casa promete/ filhos o questa firmado pola
cabeça do dragão de jupiter[38]//(f.41v) i de mars em a quinta
casa i serao estes filhos nobres/ fermosos i bem fortunados.
estando no signo de llibra/ jupiter em a septima casa dem-
ostraõ que a criaçaõ/ i conuersacaõ ordinaria deste nacido
sera em casa rreal/ constitutida sobre negocios pubricos/

A cidade de llisboa lhe sera comoda porque he sugeita
ao signo/ de libra omde jupiter se acha i serao em geral
commodos/ i proprios os becos(?)[39] que saõ sugeitos aos
signos dos peixes/ i do sagitario[40] i taõbem aquelles que saõ
debaixo de/ jupiter i uenus[41] desta nacença/

Os llugares incommodos i que deue euitar saõ estes/ que
saõ debaixo dos senhores dos signos da sexta/ oitaua i dozena
casa de saturno i mars[42] porque/ estes saõ muito incomo-
dos i contraires pera nelles/ habitar mas sede seguros disto
pollo presente; ho/ resto das elleicõis i taõbem das direicõis
i rreuolu/cõis que saõ muito necesarios pera elle i inteligen/

---

    propinquity, or by testimony are beneficent, the men get good
    wives."(395)

38   The North Node; the "Tail of the Dragon" is the South Node.

39   *beims?* or *beins?*: the reading is uncertain.

40   TB, 159, places Spain [Portugal is not mentioned separately]
    under Sagittarius.

41   TB, 425: "If Jupiter and Venus are the rulers of the places which
    govern travel … they make the journeys not only safe but also
    pleasant."

42   TB, 425: "If Saturn and Mars control the luminaries … they
    will … involve the subject in great dangers, through unfortunate
    voyages and shipwreck if they are in watery signs."

cõis do tempo i acidentes nos o rremetemos/ a outro tempo de mais uagar

fim

Appendix II

Was Sebastian the Victim of Sexual Abuse?

Deprived by fate both of a father who would be his natural protector and of a mother in whom he might confide, Sebastian, soon after his birth, was turned over to a "triumvirate" of padres[43] who saw to most of his upbringing. Although his grandmother Catherine did her best to take his mother's place,[44] she was often busy with administrative affairs and too distant from him in age to win the boy's confidence or trust. His great-uncle Henry, the Inquisitor General from 1539 on, was too occupied with his extensive duties and spent too much of his time away from the court to give much time to his grand-nephew. As a result, Sebastian was left largely unprotected: a vulnerable child, with blue eyes and reddish-blond hair, he undoubtedly would have been an attractive target for sexual abuse by unscrupulous handlers.

And indeed sexual abuse, most likely at the hands of one or more of the virtuous padres to whom his upbringing was

---

43 See note 17.

44 It was reported that she insisted that Sebastian sleep and eat in her apartments up to age seven; after that, he had his own rooms. See J. M. de Quieroz Velloso, *D. Sebastião, 1554–1578*, 2nd ed. (Lisbon, 1935) 93; hereafter "Velloso, *Sebastião*."

entrusted,[45] would explain a great deal about Sebastian that

---

45   In fact, exactly this was rumored about in 1570, when
"pasquins" (the sixteenth-century equivalent of today's *National
Enquirer*) in Coimbra claimed the King was "abarregado" with
the two brothers Câmara: Luís (his erstwhile tutor and confessor) and Martim. See Joaquim V. Serrão, *Historia de Portugal*,
III (Lisbon,1978), 65, fn. 192. Hereafter "JVS, *Historia*." The
means used to reduce Catherine's influence over her grandson
and place him almost entirely at the disposal of Câmara are
related by Alfonso Danvila y Burguero, *Don Cristobal de
de Moura, Primer Marquês de Castelo Rodrigo, 1538–1613*
(Madrid, 1900), 12–113; see also Dauril Alden, *The Making of
an Enterprise; The Society of Jesus in Portugal, its Empire and
Beyond, 1540–1750* (Stanford, 1996), 82: "the queen mother,
who came to regard Luís Gonçalves's influence upon Sebastian as ... unhealthy." Also the somewhat confused account of
Catherine's decision (later reversed) to return to Castile due to
her frustrations and dismay at her inability to alter Sebastian's
"vicious" lifestyle, which upset her mightily: Luciano Ribeiro,
"Colectânea de documentos acerca de D. Sebastião," *Stúdia*, 5
(1960), 174–175. In 1560 Luís Gonçalves became Sebastian's
confessor as well as tutor, a position he resigned—apparently
at the insistence of Dowager Queen Catherine—in 1566, soon
after Sebastian's illness first appeared. He was reinstated in
the position two years later, at Sebastian's insistence, when his
minority came to an end: Dauril Alden, *The Making of an Enterprise; The Society of Jesus in Portugal, its Empire and Beyond,
1540–1750* (Stanford, 1996), 82. This would mean that Luís
Gonçalves was acting as the king's confessor when he first came
down with his "doença" at age eleven. António Cândido Franco,
however, states that the symptoms first appeared at age ten: *Vida
de Sebastião Rei de Portugal* (Lisbon, 1993), 72. Alden, op.cit.,
discusses the hold that the Jesuits at court had upon the young
monarch (81–85), without however picking up on their possible
connection to his sexually transmitted disease. Velloso, *Sebastião*, pp, 97–98, claims that Gonçalves assumed the position
of confessor in 1566—much to the dismay of Sebastian's *aio*
Menenses, since this gave him almost complete control over his
charge. See also the ferocious attack on the brothers Câmara by
the humanist bishop Jerónimo Osório (1506–1580), in his *Cartas
Portuguesas* (Coimbra, 1922):"a linguage da gente mais graue he

has heretofore puzzled historians.[46] To begin with, it would explain the mysterious "seminal fluxes" from which he began to suffer beginning around age eleven or twelve.[47] And if, as the result of early "initiation," it lead him to a homosexual orientation,[48] much else that has puzzled historians about him would suddenly make sense. Passive anal intercourse in a young man could be one of the explanations for the difficulties he had at times in walking or riding horseback, while his difficulties in sleeping could well be one of the psychological results of such abuse.[49] A homosexual orientation would

---

têrem um Rei capitvo de dous Irmãos que pouco e pouco vam fazendo outro Rei de Ormuz." (25). The tone of the whole letter hints that their relationship with Sebastian was "unsavory."

46   Sebastian's numerous maladies have produced the most amusing collection of misdiagnoses, from "diabetic" to "epileptic" to "neuropathic," and almost everything conceivable in between. See JVS, *Historia*, 69–70; and Mário Saraiva, *Dom Sebastião na História e na Lenda* (Lisbon, 1994?). Hereafter "Saraiva, *Sebastião*."

47   J. J. Alves Dias sensibly agrees that these were the result of some type of urethritis but he errs, in my opinion, in accepting Saraiva's explanation for this: *Portugal do Renascimento à Crise Dinástica* (Lisbon,1998), 746. Any competent doctor today, confronted with symptoms of urethritis—gonococcal or not—in a preadolescent boy, would immediately suspect sexual abuse as the most likely cause. Furthermore, such diseases can cause painful swelling of the scrotum on one or both sides, as well as the eye inflammation and other complaints from which Sebastian suffered. Untreated gonorrhea, as well as other sexual diseases, would also be one logical explanation for his difficulties in riding horseback.

48   The passage in Luciano Ribeiro, "Colectânea de documentos acerca de D. Sebastião," *Stúdia*, 5 (1960), 176, would suggest that this may have been the case: "passeaua de noite cõ gente de pouca autoridade e menos mostras de uirtude."

49   "A young child who has been sexually abused may have difficulty in walking or sitting because of a physical injury ... a urinary tract infection ... may develop ... the child may be irritable ... or may sleep fitfully": see the *Merck Manual of Medical*

also be the most reasonable explanation for the obvious and unmistakable aversion to women noted by numerous observers. All this would be the most likely cause for his evasive behavior about marriage,[50] as well as the hesitations of Philip II to promise his daughter to Sebastian in marriage.

Needless to say there have been those who argue that he did not suffer from any sexually transmitted disease. Perhaps the most outspoken of these dissenters is Mário Saraiva. Bolstered by his credentials as a medical doctor,[51] Saraiva claims that Sebastian's urethritis, which he acknowledges, was merely the result of mistreatments by his physicians. And what mistreatments might these be? Well, referring to some treatises on the malady written over a century or more later—one from 1688; another from 1844[52]—Saraiva simply presumes that Sebastian was treated by invasive methods such as syringes that "turned" what was only "espermatorreia"—or "wet dreams"—into urethritis. The fact is that the only treatments administered to Sebastian that are mentioned in the sources were bleedings and the application

---

Information (Whitehouse Station, N. J., 1997), 1323; further, "If gonorrhea is not treated quickly complications may occur. In men the bacteria can spread up the urethra ... An abscess will form causing pain, fever and chills. This abscess will eventually drain which releases pus into the urethra or anus. Men may suffer from infertility ... Any form of sexual penetration (oral, anal and vaginal) can transmit gonorrhea": (www.sexhealth.org). It should be noted that Câmara was blind in one eye (see note 10), a common result of untreated gonorrhea: *The Merck Manual of Medical Information* (Whitehouse Station, NJ, 1997), 942: "In adults ... often only one eye is affected. Blindness may result if the infection isn't treated."

50   Untreated urethritis can leave the victim impotent. If that were the case with Sebastian, obviously marriage and the attendant revelation of his condition would be unthinkable.

51   Saraiva apparently received a degree in medicine from the University of Coimbra in 1936.

52   François Foy, *Formulaire des médecins praticiens* (Paris, 1844).

of "emplastos."[53] Nothing else: no syringes, no "lavatórios deffecativos,"[54] nor anything else gratuitously imagined by Saraiva. Thus what we have here, in my view, is a transparent attempt to whitewash an unpleasant and embarrassing situation in order to avoid the most obvious explanation: that at about the age of eleven, Sebastian contracted gonorrhea[55] due to sexual abuse. This is the only reasonable explanation for his "seminal effusions," as well as a number of his other ailments.[56]

In conclusion, although we cannot state it as a proven fact, the hypothesis that Sebastian was the victim of sexual abuse—and as a result most likely developed a homosexual orientation—provides so reasonable and convincing an explanation for his physical and psychological maladies that it must to be carefully weighed by any future biographer of this unfortunate young man and ill-fated king.[57]

---

53   Velloso, *Sebastião*, 104.

54   How a rectal lavage, even if it were administered, could possibly turn "wet dreams"("espermatorreia") into urethritis Dr. Saraiva fails to explain to us.

55   Indeed, doctors specifically called his illness gonorrhea: "une secrette maladie qu'on appelle gonorrée, à laquelle il est subject." (Velloso, *Sebastião*, 107). They, of course, did not understand its etiology but knew it, so to speak, when they saw it.

56   Even Velloso, *Sebastião*, 107, who accepts the idea that he had a sexually transmitted infection, would prefer to believe that it was contracted "indirectly," though he fails to offer any explanation why this would have been more likely than direct transmission.

57   The attempt of Francisco Rodrigues, *História da Companhia de Jesus na Assistência de Portugal*, II:2 (Porto, 1939), 329–338, to refute this explanation can be dismissed as tendentious. Clearly, a twentieth-century Jesuit historian could not be expected to entertain—much less endorse—the idea that a Portuguese king, even in the sixteenth century, might have been sexually molested by Jesuit *padres* of the court. The rest of Rodrigues's examination of Sebastian's unsuccessful marriage negotiations is unconvincing: he fails to pick up on the large amount of evidence presented by disinterested observers about Sebastian's profound dislike of

Appendix III

Bull of Sixtus V vs. Judicial Astrology (1586)

Against those practicing the art of judicial astrology, and any other types of divination, and against those reading or having books about these subjects.[58]

Bishop Sixtus V, Servant of the servants of God

Although God the Omnipotent One, creator of Heaven and Earth, gave to man—whom He created in his own image and likeness—a mind colored by the divine light of faith so that he might not only know the mysteries which surpass human reason, but might also, albeit with difficulty, look into and know many magnificent things, nonetheless he made him in

---

women, as well as the "hold" that the brothers Câmara had over him. He likewise fails to understand that they had no need to "prevent" his marriage: the misogynic orientation of the personality they had crafted took care of that matter by itself with no need for further intervention from them. Finally, failing, as he does, to understand that it was sexually transmitted, Rodrigues appears to be just as confused about Sebastian's *doença* as were some of his doctors—though not Philip II or Catherine de Medici.

58   Edited and freely translated from the Latin text in *Bullarium Privilegiorum ac Diplomatum romanorum Pontificum Amplissima Collectio, ... tomus quartus, pars quarta, ab anno X. GREGORII XIII usque ad annum III. SIXTI V, scilicet ab anno 1581 ad 1588* (Rome, 1747), 176–179.

such a way that he might comprehend such profound matters not as a haughty animal, but rather so that he would fear, and, prostrate on the ground, venerate the immense majesty of his maker. To Himself alone did God reserve the knowledge of those things that will come to pass and the awareness of future matters. For it is He alone, before whose eyes all things are naked and transparent, who sees through to the deepest thoughts of men and consequently understands their actions; it is He alone who calls upon those things which are not yet in existence as if they were in existence; it is He alone who beholds all things present and set out before his eyes; and finally it is He alone who knows all things from the beginning of time and for all eternity. And with wondrous providence has He created these things that are unknown not only to the human mind in its frailty, but even to evil spirits themselves before they come to pass. Thus, in the book of Isaiah, the Holy Spirit mocks the falsity and foolishness of idols in revealing future events—and the vanity of those who give credence to them—with these words: "Proclaim what things are to be in the future, and we will know them because you are Gods." In the New Testament, Christ our Lord turned aside the inquiries of His disciples who were persistently asking about future events with this answer, which in fact He used to repress the curiosity of all His faithful: "It is not for you to know the times, or the instances, which the Father in his power has established." Nor indeed are there any true ways or methods for knowing future events and chance circumstances beforehand—necessarily leaving out future events known from natural causes, or those known from common occurrences which have nothing to do with divination. All those ways and methods are false and empty because they come from the tricks of evil spirits, from whose action, advice, or aid every type of divination springs. Indeed, they know these things not through any divine quality, nor from a true knowledge of future things, but by the keenness of their craftier natures and by certain other means of which the dull knowledge of men does not perceive. For this reason, it must not be doubted that in seeking the precognition of chance circumstances and important things to come, the devil acts with false intent so that by his deceptions and tricks he may turn men away from the path of salvation and trap them in the snare of damnation.

Even though these things are as they are, some faithful and religious persons, not giving much thought to it but eagerly pursuing curious matters, do grave offense to God, going astray themselves and sending others into error. Most notable of these are the astrologers once called mathematicians, the readers of birth signs, and those persons called *Planetarii*—who, making a show of their false knowledge of the stars and constellations, and most rashly busying themselves to anticipate the decree of the divine order which will in its own time be revealed, make predictions with regard to expectant mothers or the birthdays of men according to the movement of the constellations or the course of the stars. They pass judgments on future or present events, as well as things hidden in the past, and they presume to have precognition and to make rash predictions from the births of children ... concerning their [future] status, circumstances, courses of life, offices, riches, offspring, salvation, death, journeys, struggles, enmities, imprisonments, slaughters, various crises, and other events good and bad. And not without great danger of error and infidelity do they do this. Saint Augustine, the esteemed light of the Church, makes clear that anyone who takes heed of these things or studies them, or who takes these persons into his home or looks for truth in them, has violated baptism and the Christian faith. He accuses them rightly, and upbraids them with these words: "Pay attention to the days and months and seasons and years. I fear that perhaps I have labored on your behalf for no good reason." Therefore these very rash and petty men—to the wretched destruction of their souls, the downfall of the faithful, and the detriment of the

Christian faith—attribute to the stars and constellations the future outcomes of things, and whatever will come to pass for good or ill: in short, those things which ultimately issue from the free will of men. They attribute to the stars and constellations the ability or the power to make known future things, and on this basis they do not hesitate to make judgments concerning all these matters and to sell these predictions openly. A few people—unsophisticated, lacking in experience and good sense, and too trusting in others—give such great faith to these men that on account of ... judgments and predictions of this sort, they believe or hope that something is certain to take place. Truly the foolishness of these people, as well as the credulity of their unfortunate disciples, must be particularly deplored. Though warned by divine writings, they do not understand the excellence of man: the Heavens, and the Stars, and the brightest constellations of the sky, the Sun and Moon ... do not give commands, but rather they serve man. For thus did Moses forewarn the people of God to beware of this error: "Do not, by chance with eyes elevated to the sky, look upon the Sun and Moon and all the stars of the Sky, and, deceived by error, worship and adore those things which your Lord God created to give aid to all the races which exist below the sky." But why is it so surprising that the constellations serve man? Are not the Angels themselves sent to aid those who receive the birthright of salvation? For it so pleased God that he ordained not only Bishops, just as it was written by St. Ambrose, to watch over his flock of right-thinking sheep, but he even set aside Angels for that purpose. Indeed, Saint Jerome expresses it very well: "The great dignity of every soul is that each has, from birth, an angel chosen to be its guardian." But if Angels guard men, what can stars, which are by no means to be compared to Angels, do or achieve in comparison to the guardianship and tutelage of Angels? Nor indeed, at this point, should we pass over the statement of an outstanding doctor of the church, the most blessed Pope

Gregory the Great, who with the great weight of his words confutes the Priscillian heretics for thinking that each man is born under sway of the constellations: "Let it be no part of the hearts of the faithful to say that anything is 'fate.' Indeed, a single builder, who created the lives of men, watches over them. Indeed, man was not made for the sake of stars, but stars were made for the sake of man."

It has long since been established by the rules of the Index of forbidden books, according to the decree of the Holy Ecumenical Council held at Trent, that Bishops should diligently watch out ... lest books, handbooks, and indices about this sort of judicial astrology be read or possessed.

We, therefore, who in accordance with the duty of our Pastoral office must preserve the integrity of the faith inviolate—and who wish ... as far as we are able, with the help of divine grace, to look after the safety of souls—condemn and rebuke all types of divination that usually arise from the Devil in order to deceive the faithful. We desire moreover, that the holy innocence of the Christian Religion ... be ... kept whole and uncorrupted from every slip of error. Therefore we establish and command, by virtue of ... our apostolic authority and in accordance with Church discipline, that to the same degree as in the past ... bishops, prelates, and superiors, as well as inquisitors of heretical depravity, diligently seek out and take harsh action against astrologers, mathematicians, and any others practicing the astrological arts who make predictions concerning agriculture, navigation, the art of magic, and birth charts of men or dare to affirm anything yet to take place concerning important future events, chance occurrences, or actions that depend upon human will—even if they claim or testify to the effect that they did not affirm it as a certainty. Let the men of the Church turn their minds to the judgment of these persons, irrespective of whatever station, rank, or kind they may be.

Therefore we prohibit each and every book, work, and

treatise of judiciary astrology, geomancy, hydromancy, pyromancy, onomancy, chiromancy, necromancy, and the art of magic, or in which fortune-telling, potions, augury, omens, accursed chants, and superstitions are contained, and just as in the Index mentioned above, those forbidden to be read by any of the Christian faithful under penalty of the censures and punishments contained in that Index. All those books ought to be handed over and registered by bishops, the local church authorities, or the aforementioned inquisitors. And to no lesser degree, we decree and command by the same authority that in similar fashion the same inquisitors are free and permitted to take action against those who knowingly read or keep books and writings of this sort and to confine and punish them with appropriate punishments.

Moreover, in order that our present writings may more easily be brought to the common attention of all, we order them to be affixed or hung on the folding doors of the Lateran Basilica of St. John, from the city of the first of the Apostles, and on the edge of the plain of Flora, and should they be torn down, we order printed copies of them to be left attached in the same places.

In addition, we command each and every one of our venerable brothers patriarch, cardinals, archbishops, bishops, local priests and prelates, and of course the inquisitors of heretical wrongdoing everywhere that, in accordance with the virtue of holy obedience, they—after they have received or taken notice of these decrees—will, through their own agency or that of others, make these same decrees public in an ordinary sermon or whenever a great number of people has convened for the purpose of divine services. This will be done once a year, or as often as seems to be useful.

Given in Rome at Saint Peter's, in the year of the incarnation of our Lord 1586, on the Nones of January in the first year of our current pontificate.

A Pedophile in the Palace

or

The Sexual Abuse of King Sebastian of Portugal (1554–1578) and Its Consequences[1]

> Llorò el pueblo Lusitano para tenerle,
> y llorò porque le tuvo—
>> Manuel Faria y Sousa,
>> *Epitome de las Historias Portuguesas*

Portuguese independence hung in the balance during the first weeks of January of 1554. The reigning King, João III (r. 1521–1557), had sired no fewer than nine children—six of them male—but by 1554 all but one of them, the prince also named João, were dead.[2] This only surviving heir to the

---

1 A Portuguese version appeared in *Dois Estudos Polémicos* (Tucson; Fenestra, 2004), 47–83. Reprinted with permission and minor alterations.

2 For the reign of João III, see now the brief but up-to-date overview of Paulo Drumond Braga, *D. João III* (Lisbon, 2002), unfortunately published without an index or genealogical tables.

43

gravely ill king had been betrothed two years earlier, in 1552, at age fifteen, to the sister of Philip II of Spain, Doña Juana of Austria, age seventeen. The two youngsters soon discovered an intense sexual attraction for each other, and Juana had become pregnant around the end of April of 1553.[3] But by the close of that same year, Prince João himself fell gravely ill with juvenile diabetes, from which he died shortly afterward on January 2, 1554. Thus the only remaining heir to the terminally ill João III, king of Portugal, was still in the womb of his recently widowed daughter-in-law, Doña Juana. Only her successful delivery of a healthy child stood between Portuguese independence and almost certain deliverance of the nation into the control of its detested Castilian neighbor.[4] Thus it is understandable that the course of her pregnancy was followed with intense concern:

> ... God having willed the death of so many children, the prince and only heir to the kingdom ... married at age sixteen [sic] with the princess Dona Juana daughter of the glorious emperor Charles V ... But His Divine Majesty ordained that a mortal illness [juvenile diabetes] would carry off this prince, thus leaving the hope of a succession to the kingdom hanging by a thin thread, [so] great care was taken that the princess would not hear of the death of her husband whom. . . she loved with an intense [strange]

---

3 João was so persistent, it is said, that his doctors finally thought this might be the cause of his illness and that the two should be separated: "... *demasiada comunicação, e amor, com que se havia com a Princeza.*" D. Manuel de Meneses, *Chronica do Muito Alto, e Muito Esclarecido Principe D. Sebastião* (Lisbon, 1730), I, chapter 6. Therefore in November of 1553, the newlyweds were separated, and Juana went to live in the apartments of her aunt and mother-in-law, Queen Catarina. (See genealogical table.)

4 See footnote 27.

affection. [Then there came] ... the fateful hour when the desired birth pangs of the princess arrived a little after midnight of the 20th of January of the year 1554 ... the festive day of the glorious Saint Sebastian ...

And as word of this spread about the city, it was "ordered that there take place a devout procession by the religious orders and the clergy from the city cathedral to the monastery of São Domingos carrying with it the arm of the glorious saint [Sebastian] that had been brought to this kingdom at the time of the sack of Rome." Meanwhile

... with unrestrained feeling people left their houses irrespective of estate, age or quality of person and at the sacred altars [of the city] cried to God with constant tears on behalf of the only hope for this Crown. The palace square was filled with citizens their eyes glued to the Palace verandas toward which they stared in silence with their spirits on hold when just before daybreak there appeared at the windows and verandas Nobles and Ladies who stumbling over their words from excessive joy announced the happy news that the Princess had given birth to a prince for Portugal ...[5]

In gratitude for his safe delivery, the young prince, born around 8:15 a.m., was named Sebastian after the saint on whose day he came into the world.[6]

---

5   Luciano Ribeiro, "Colectânea de Documents Acerca de D. Sebastião," *Stúdia*, V (1960), 168–69. The time of his birth was later, however; see footnote 6.

6   Manuel J. Gandra, *Joaquim de Fiore, Joaquimismo e Esperança Sebástica* (Lisbon: Fundação Lusíada, 1999), 86, commenting upon a rudimentary nativity for Sebastian found in João Baptista

Not long after his birth, a Castilian physician in attendance on this mother, Dr. Fernão (Fernando or Fernán) Abarca Maldonado, cast the infant's horoscope. Relying closely, almost slavishly, upon Ptolemy's *Tetrabiblos*,[7] and using the time, date, and location of his birth as coordinates, he cast the infant prince's horoscope to inform the royal court of what lay in store for him.[8] Some of Maldonado's predictions came true, while others (such as that he would have a dark complexion and hair and black eyes) did not. In fact tossing a coin or pure chance would likely have done as well. And salient among the physician's less felicitous predictions were those regard-

---

Lavanha's *Relação das Coisas que Sucederam no Tempo de el-Rei D. Sebastião* (1602?) says he was born at 7:18 AM. This is clearly wrong; not only does it contradict the testimony of Francisco de Andrada, *Chrónica de D. João III*, ed. M. Lopes de Almeida (Porto, 1976), 1192, but also the clear information in Maldonado's horoscope, probably cast very shortly after his birth. Quite inexplicably Isabel Braga in her recent study of Portuguese/ Spanish interrelations in the first half of the sixteenth century says Sebastian was born *fourteen* (sic) days after the death of his father, thus making the sixteenth of January his birth date: Isabel Drumond Braga, *Um Espaço, Duas Monarquias (Interrelações na Península Ibérica no Tempo de Carlos V)* (Lisbon, 2001), 248.

7   This was the astrological manual written by Claudius Ptolemy, the Alexandrine astronomer-geographer of the second century AD that Maldonado used as a guide for his commentary on Sebastian's horoscope. See Ptolemy, *Tetrabiblos*, ed. and trans. by F. E. Robbins (Cambridge: Harvard University Press, 1998), passim. It is likely that Maldonado used a Latin translation of Ptolemy and not the Greek original.

8   Predicting one's future by means of a horoscope was technically a violation of church law, since it infringed upon free will and usurped God's exclusive power to know and see the future, but nonetheless it took place with great regularity. See the bull "Terrae et Coeli Creator" (1586) of Pope Sixtus V that outlaws the practice in *Bullarium Privilegiorum ac Diplomatum romanorum Pontificum Amplissima Collectio, IV:4, ab anno X GREGORII XIII usque ad annum III. SIXTI V, scilicet ab anno 1581 ad 1588* (Rome, 1747), 176–79.

ing Sebastian's sex life, that is to say, his relationships with women and his expected marriage. Here is what Maldonado said he found in casting Sebastian's horoscope:

> I say that this newborn will be very much given to his pleasures with women ... The moon in the eastern quarter says that he will marry in his youth and his wife will be a good and honest woman as is indicated by Jupiter being in the Seventh House. Although Venus in Capricorn gives him a great inclination toward sexual activity, this will be in the context of a lawful marriage. The time for this will be found by the directions of Venus and Venus in the Eleventh House gives promise of sons which is confirmed by the Head of the Dragon of Jupiter and Mars in the Fifth House says these sons will be handsome, noble, and lucky. [9]

In short the young king would have a strong interest in the opposite sex and be married early in life to a "good" woman by whom he would have many children. This welcome prediction seemed certain to guarantee the future of Portugal as an independent kingdom. Unfortunately all of these predictions of Maldonado's horoscope turned out to be completely

---

9   There is a Portuguese translation of the bull in Harold Johnson, *Camponeses e Colonizadores* (Lisbon, 2002), 163–66.

"... *digo que este nacido sera muito dado a seus prazeres como a molheres ... A lluã em aquarta parte oriental diz que elle sera casado em sua mocidade i sera sua molher boa e honesta que he significada por jupiter em a septima casa ... Aimda que venus no signo de capricornio lha daa inclinacaõ gramde nas cousas uenereas. Aimda que esto sera com ligitimo matrimonio. o tempo do qual se achara pelas dirreiçõens i as emcerra uenus e na omezena casa promete filhos o questa firmado pola cabeça do dragão de jupiter e de mars em a quinta casa I serao este filhos nobres fermosos e bem fortunados.*" See Johnson, *Camponeses*, 156–57.

wrong. In reality Sebastian was a vast disappointment to a people hoping for a king whose marriage would reestablish the royal lineage and thus protect the independence of the country. Not only was he unmistakably misogynic, but he managed to wiggle skillfully and determinedly out of every potential marriage alliance that could be arranged for him.[10] The result was, of course, a king without offspring who then went on to bring the Portuguese royal house to an end with his death twenty-four years later in the ill-fated battle of Alcázar Kebir.

Portuguese historians consequently have been unsympathetic, even harsh, in their judgments of Sebastian, though few have been quite so intemperate as the usually serene polymath, António Sérgio. Here is Sérgio's vitriolic assessment of Sebastian and his reign:

> It is not exactly his imprudence that we deplore in King Sebastian but the stupidity, the silliness, the explosive morbidity, the pointless ferocity, the

---

10   See, for example, the letter sent to him in 1569 by his mother: "Señor. According to what my brother [Philip II of Spain] and Dom Francisco Pereira have told me, I am aware of the reply that you have given to His Majesty [Philip II] who wrote to you about the power [legal power to act on his behalf] that you need to send to finalize and conclude your marriage, and I cannot but be very astonished at your procrastination with regard to this matter that is already so advanced, and after everything has been arranged as you wished, since there could be many problems if Your Majesty does not do without delay what my brother has written asking you to do ... I very much ask Your Majesty not to permit any more procrastination but that you immediately send the power to D. Francisco Pereira, as I expect you will, seeing the reasons there are for no more delay ...": Diogo Barbosa Machado, *Memórias para a Historia de Portugal, que Comprehendem o Governo del Rey D. Sebastião* (Lisbon Occidental, 1747), v. III, 116–17. Of course the power was never sent, and the marriage never took place.

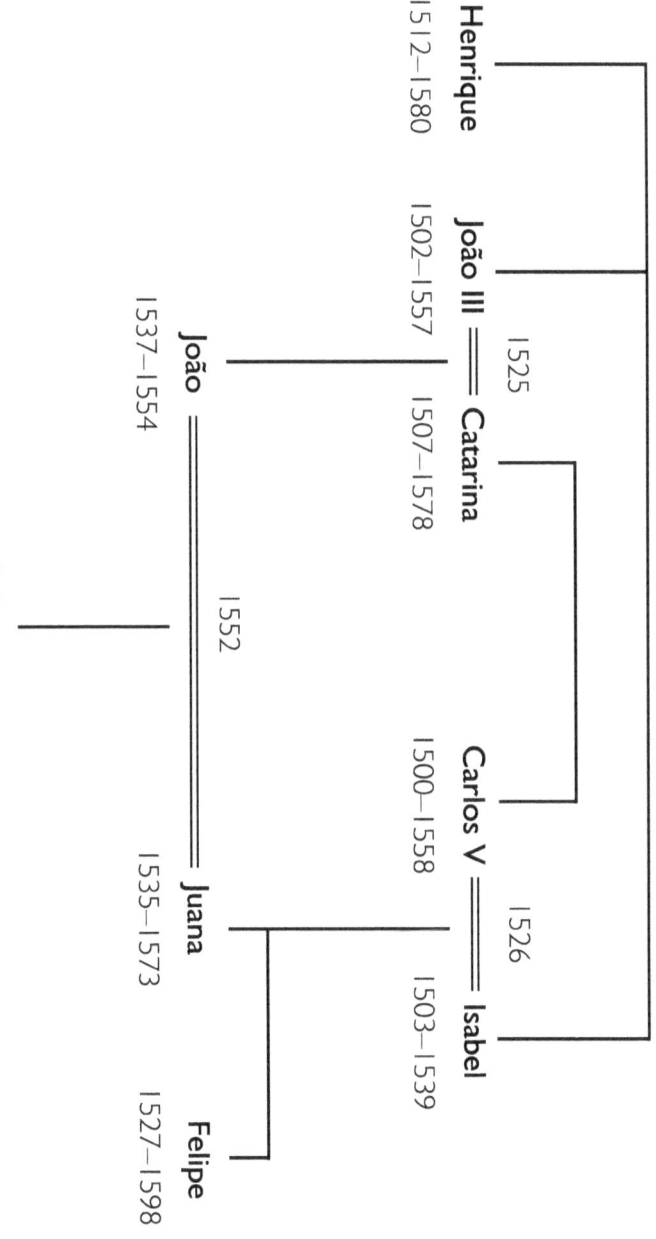

Genealogical Table

constant idiocy of this impulsive degenerate who was completely devoid of the qualities of command indispensable for the execution of what he aspired to do. If, for example, chance had given him victory at Alcázar Kebir, soon other asinine actions would have finished him off, since the gift of perpetually spouting forth asininities was a congenital defect in this young man.[11]

Thus was young Sebastian excoriated as stupid, nutty, silly, and impulsive—in sum a "degenerate" out of whom "asinine behavior spouted in a perpetual jet." Elsewhere Sérgio was even more blunt, calling Sebastian "that unsurpassed piece of an ass" (*"esse inexcedível pedaço de asno"*).[12] While not going to quite the same lengths as Sérgio, few other Portuguese historians have come to Sebastian's defense. By and large, he is viewed unsympathetically by most of those who recount his reign.

This can be seen from a review of the various assessments of Sebastian to be found in some major recent general histories of Portugal.[13] We will choose four as representative: those

---

11   António Sérgio, *Breve Interpretação da História de Portugal*, 13th ed. (Lisbon, 1989), 104: *"Não é pròpriamente a imprudência o que deploramos em D. Sebastião, mas a estupidez, o desvairamento, a tontaria, a explosividade mórbida, a ferocidade inútil, a pataratice constante desse impulsivo degenerado, que era de todo destituído das qualidades de comando absolutamente indispensáveis para a execução do que ambicionava. Se um acaso, por exemplo. lhe desse a vitória em Alcácer Quibir, logo outras asneiras o haveriam perdido, porque o dom da asneira em jacto contínuo era nesse jovem uma propriedade congénita."*

12   António Sérgio, *Ensaios*, I (Lisbon, 1971), 241.

13   On the other hand, a recent biography by the Spanish historian, António Villacorta Baños-García, *Don Sebastián, rey de Portugal* (Barcelona, 2001), is considerably better, although still unable to give a clear indication of what his *"rara* [sic]*enfermedad"* (88) was or how he got it.

of Joaquim Veríssimo Serrão (1978); of Francisco de Sales Loureiro (1983); of Joaquim Romero Magalhães (1993); and of João Alves Dias, written in collaboration with Isabel and Paulo Braga (1998).

J. V. Serrão notes that Sebastian and his reign, in spite of all that has been written on the topic, are still matters of debate, especially due to his importance as the symbol of the loss of Portuguese independence. He goes on to opine that in order to produce a definitive study there are still lacking the "indispensable mental tools" that ought to include an understanding of the young king's personal impulses and motivations. Serrão concludes, "We believe that the history of Sebastian that will be erected some day will have to be more psychological than documental." He further points out that Sebastian's correspondence reveals him to be "confused, almost never responding to questions put [to him]" and speaks as well of his "affective frigidity that explains his reluctance to get married"—if his "strange illness" does not already explain that. In sum Serrão is of the view that Sebastian never married due to his "precarious health, psychological perturbations and lack of motivation." He also thinks Sebastian's illness contributed to his "unbalanced personality, lack of good sense, impulsiveness, inability to reflect as well as his capricious demand for obedience." One should note that while Serrão clearly believes that Sebastian's illness is the cause of most of the "oddities" of his personality and problems of his reign, he never ventures to say what it might be, limiting himself to calling it "strange," and offers no clue where it may have come from. [14]

Some five years later, in 1983, Francisco de Sales de Mascarenhas Loureiro, already known for his earlier work on Sebastian, attempted a general survey of the reign for

14   Joaquim Veríssimo Serrão, *História de Portugal*, III (Lisbon, 1978), 68–70.

the history edited by José Hermano Saraiva.[15] He explains
that many of Sebastian's actions resulted from what he terms
his "psychological alterations" that came from having been
born after his father had died and to a mother who left him
when only three months old in the care of a grandmother and
a granduncle. With regard to Sebastian's failure to marry, he
recognizes that a "certain historigraphical current" blames
Luís Gonçalves da Câmara (Sebastian's tutor/confessor)
as the "moral [sic] author" of Sebastian's misogyny or
misogamy. But this idea, he claims, is refuted by the account
of his life by Padre Amador Rebelo. For Loureiro, therefore,
it was not the brothers Câmara or the Jesuits who prevented
Sebastian from marrying, but rather his uncle Philip II. In
fact Loureiro never comes to grips at all with the question
of Sebastian's illness nor how he contracted it, nor much of
anything else about his personality that was certainly not
the model of normality suggested by Loureiro's account. [16]

Ten years later, in 1993, another sixteenth-century specialist, Joaquim Romero Magalhães, turned his attention
to Sebastian in the section he wrote for the multivolume
history edited by José Mattoso. Sebastian's defects of char-

---

15   Francisco de Sales Loureiro, "D. Sebastião e Alcácer Quibir," in
     História de Portugal, dir., José Hermano Saraiva (Lisbon: Alfa,
     1983), IV, 134–38.

16   Rebelo was a close ally of the brothers Câmara at the court and
     strove to portray them in a very favorable light. See Francisco
     Sales Loureiro, O Padre Luís Gonçalves da Câmara e D. Sebas-
     tião (Coimbra, 1973), 22, where the author expresses astonish-
     ment that "there are even some who do not hesitate to claim the
     Monarch suffered from a sexual disease, provoked by a preco-
     cious experience!" He then goes on to brush this aside with the
     remark "however that may be" and later refers to the "very con-
     tinent spirit" of "our sovereign," implying that Sebastian was not
     infected with anything, merely asexual. But elsewhere he refers
     to Philip II's anxiety to find a husband for Isabel Clara Eugénia
     "without the illness of a sexual nature that our King revealed."
     Thus Loureiro leaves the whole matter in confusion and doubt.

acter are attributed here to his having been inundated from childhood with references to his long hoped for and miraculous birth. These left him feeling immune to the accidents of fortune and unwilling to settle for the role of a bureaucratic administrative king. In addition, opines Magalhães, his "almost incestuous lineage" probably produced some "genetic defects." With no father or mother present, and brought up without much control by complacent grandparents, he was turned by his Jesuit teachers into a religious zealot and anti-Muslim crusader long after the crusades. Magalhães never discusses Sebastian's odd absence of a sex life or his physical malady beyond a casual mention that he avoided marrying due "possibly to illness or misogyny." That is all that he says about that—in short, precious little. But since the king's failure to marry or beget children was absolutely crucial for his reign as well as for Portugal's future, the author's facile dismissal of these questions is odd indeed and shows how very loath Portuguese historiography has been to "peek under the carpet" to get a better grasp on the truth.[17]

Five years after Magalhães, another account of Sebastian and his reign appeared in the *Nova História de Portugal* series (edited by Joel Serrão and A. H. de Oliveira Marques) that was written by three historians conjointly.[18] This summary of Sebastian and his reign attributes his "difficult behavior" to a "certain psychological imbalance" and "deficiencies in his education" as well as to the genetic results of repeated intermarriages, but clears him of being an epileptic or diabetic. Still, with regard to his penile discharges that cannot be

---

17   Joaquim Romero Magalhães, "D. Sebastião," in *História de Portugal*, dir, José Mattoso (Lisbon: Círculo de Leitores, 1993), 540–46.

18   J. J. Alves Dias, *Portugal do Renascimento à Crise Dinástica* (Lisbon, 1998), 741–52.

denied, these are minimized by claiming they were merely "wet dreams" (*espermatorreia*) and nothing more.[19]

It is obvious that all these accounts, written over a twenty-year period from 1978 to 1998, clearly beat about the bush, never coming to grips with the fundamental issues, in spite of the fact that these were made perfectly clear by Queirós Velloso in the chapter he wrote over seventy years ago, in 1933, for the Barcelos history of Portugal.[20] Indeed one might well say

---

19   This casual dismissal of his symptoms (based on the faulty ideas of Mário Saraiva) has been refuted already by Johnson in his study of Sebastian's horoscope: Johnson, *Camponeses*, 161. In addition to the arguments adduced there, it should be noted that in the 1630s, Portuguese youths thought that one was too young at twelve years of age to produce semen (David Higgs, "Lisbon" in David Higgs, *Queer Sites: Gay Urban Histories Since 1600* [London, 1999], 117). If one could not produce semen at age twelve in the seventeenth century, it is virtually certain that the same was true in the sixteenth. Thus the "fluxes" that Sebastian experienced at age ten were without any doubt due to a sexually transmitted disease and not to a normal nighttime discharge of semen ("wet dreams" or, in Portuguese, *espermatorreia*). Even today when health is generally better and sexual development takes place sooner, semen normally begins to be produced between the ages of twelve and a half and fourteen: *Merck Manual of Medical Information* (Whitehouse Station, NJ, 1997), 1255.

20   J. M. de Queiroz Velloso, "História Política," in *História de Portugal*, dir. Damião Peres, (Barcelos, 1933) V, 53–59. The Velloso chapter gets to the heart of matters very well. He even refutes the idea that Sebastian's "seminal fluxes" were merely "wet dreams" with the comment that if they were, he would have been marvelously "precocious" to have them at age ten. He in fact accepts that Sebastian probably had a sexually transmitted disease, but claims that it must have been "indirectly" acquired, since "everything we know of his life argues against direct contagion." He then drops the matter, saying that the "classification and study" of the illness "doesn't belong here." As argued earlier, almost everything written on the matter since Velloso has been backtracking in an attempt to whitewash or pretty up the unpleasant truth. Whether the Velloso chapter benefited from

that most of the work on Sebastian in the seventy years since 1933 has simply backpedaled on what Velloso had achieved in understanding the child and his reign, the backpedaling done in an apparent attempt to somehow varnish the facts to make them "nicer" and cover up the truth rather than pursuing it to its proper conclusion. The Velloso chapter, although it makes no attempt to determine the exact cause of Sebastian's illness, is more than explicit enough about what it was for any person (even slightly knowledgeable) to perceive that it was a sexually transmitted disease, almost certainly gonorrhea or chlamydia, possibly both. Drawing on Danvila y Burguero's richly informative biography of Cristobal de Moura[21] and the copious correspondence from Castilian agents at the Portuguese court on which the book is based, Velloso spells out the course of Sebastian's malady in considerable detail. First appearing at age ten, it never left him for the rest of his life.[22] This would immediately undermine any idea that it

---

the fact that in 1932–1933 the Salazar regime had not become firmly established and the repressive intellectual atmosphere of the next forty years not yet been firmly consolidated is not immediately clear. Certainly after 1933 it was probably unthinkable in Portugal to argue that Sebastian suffered from a sexually transmitted disease or, yet more unthinkable, was the victim of sexual abuse by a Jesuit father. Today (2003), however, and especially since the revelations that there have been decades of ongoing pedophilic abuse of boys at the Casa Pia orphanage in Lisbon, there may be more willingness to entertain such "unthinkable" thoughts in Portugal.

21   Alfonso Davila Y Burguero, *Don Cristobal de Moura, Primer Marquês de Castelo Rodrigo, 1538–1613* (Madrid, 1900).

22   Although most historians say that Sebastian's infection began shortly after his eleventh birthday, there is good reason to think it appeared earlier, when he was ten. Camara wrote in February of 1566 that the "mal" had begun more than two years before, but that it had been more generally known for only one year, and that no one was able to determine what it was. See Francisco Rodrigues, S. J., *História da Companhia de Jesus na Assistencia de Portugal*, II;2 (Porto, 1938), 338, fn. 1. That Camara claims to

was merely wet dreams or a urethritis caused by some aggres-
sive medical treatments. Furthermore the constant reports on
the vicissitudes of the disease, its exacerbations as well as
its remittances, that Philip II's agents sent to Madrid make it
clear that it was chronic and uncured. Instead of picking up
on Velloso's information and pursuing it, Portuguese historians went to work to deny it and to explain it away. Two mile-
stones in this effort are a book by Mário Saraiva and a long
article by Joaquim de Moura Relvas.

Moura Relvas' study, described by Sales Loureiro as
"very well structured" ("*muito bem estruturado*") and "fur-
nishing information that fits perfectly with the results of the
most recent historical investigation" ("*fornecendo dados que
se adequam perfeitamente com os resultados da mais actual-
izada investigação histórica*") is in fact highly comical to a
minimally informed reader of today. The naïveté of his arguments make it unnecessary to detail them here. Let us simply
say that, apparently an advocate of the somatic and phreno-
logical diagnosis of illnesses, he spends many pages analyz-
ing paintings of Sebastian in which he finds, not quirks of
the painters, but rather clear evidences of Sebastian's health
and virility or lack thereof. He concludes that Sebastian's
penile discharges were nothing more than a banal urethritis
that became chronic since it "installed itself" in a "diabetic
terrain."[23]

---

have known about it a full year before others lends weight to the
suspicion that he was the agent of its transmission and kept the
information to himself. Among previous commentators, António
Cândido Franco, *Vida de Sebastião Rei de Portugal* (Lisbon,
1993), 73, is the only one to claim, correctly in my view, that the
symptoms first appeared when he was ten.

23   Sales Loureiro, *Sebastião*, 137; Joaquim de Moura-Relvas,
"El-Rei Dom Sebastião," *O Instituto*, CXXXV (1972), 23–151.
A few of Moura-Relvas's diagnoses will serve to reveal his
approach: "*A fronte olímpica, patente em D. João III ... indicia
heredo-sífilis* [33]; *Na gravura* [of Sebastian] *de Jerónimo Cock*

Another investigator, Mário Saraiva, armed with some medical credentials, also goes to great lengths to refute any idea that Sebastian had a sexually transmitted disease. Drawing upon his expertise, such as it may have been, as a graduate in medicine from the University of Coimbra in 1936, he undertakes to tell us what we need to know about Sebastian's health. To his mind, Sebastian's urethritis (which he acknowledges) was merely the result of mistreatments by his physicians. And what were these erroneous treatments? Taking as his point of departure some medical treatises on the malady written over a century or more later (one from 1688; the other from 1844)[24] he anachronistically argues that

---

salta à vista a fronte olímpica dando abaulamento da testa que pode estar relacionado com a hiperostose do osso frontal que se manifesta em casos de raquitismo curado ou heredo-sífilis."(116); "...*a órbita esquerda está num plano superior ao da direita e ...o lábio inferior é espesso e pendente, mas a fácies é mesoprósopa e não leptoprósopa. Também não há indícios de prognatismo inferior. Os botões do gibão formam uma curva de convexidade esqueda, sugerindo a existência de escoliose lombar. Nota-se depois a forte saliência dos órgãos genitais externos excessivamente volumosos para a idade de 11 anos*" (116). Later on, "*A associação de polifagia com a polidipsia de D. Sebastião sugere diabetes*" (118). The salient codpieces visible in paintings of him causes Moura-Relvas to pronounce him "*bem dotado.*" Yet if one compares his size to that of his cousin Don Carlos, Sebastian suffers by comparison. Furthermore the size of a codpiece need have very little to do with the size of its contents; even Moura Relvas should have known that.

24   António Gonçalves, *Tratado da Gonorreia* (1688); François Foy, *Traité de Matière Médicale et de Thérapeutique Appliquée à Chaque Maladie en Particulier* (Paris, 1843). Works by Dr. Foy can be found in a number of libraries, but it would seem that this particular one is to be found only in the French National Library. It is not in the libraries of Yale, Harvard, the University of California, the University of Chicago, or the Library of Congress. The work of Gonçalves is not in any major library, including the British Library, the Biblioteca Nacional of Lisbon, or the Biblioteca Nacional of Madrid, that I can discover. Saraiva claims to

Sebastian was treated by "invasive" methods (syringes, etc.) that "turned" what was only "wet dreams" (*"espermatorreia"*) into urethritis. In fact the sources tell us what treatments Sebastian received. He was bled often (and this would explain his repeated attacks of vertigo) and had plasters *(emplastos)* applied, plus being given "syrup of endive" to drink to cool his liver.[25] There is nothing whatsoever to indicate that the syringes or rectal lavages (*"lavatórios deffecativos"*) imagined by Saraiva were ever employed and, even if they were, how they could turn "wet dreams" into urethritis is far from clear. Apparently for Relvas and Saraiva it was simply impossible, a priori, to believe that Sebastian might suffer from something so socially embarrassing as a sexually transmitted disease, and therefore he did not.

In short, since 1933, or for the last seventy years, Portuguese historiography has been engaged in an effort to muddy the waters about Sebastian and his illness, all in an attempt to run away from some unpleasant facts that do not "look good." The idea that a young king could be the victim of sexual abuse in the palace is apparently just too outlandish for Portuguese historians to accept.

Thus, to date, there has been no advance in the study of Sebastian himself in contrast to some excellent work on the events of his reign.[26] As a result, the life of King Sebastian of Portugal is in need of a thorough-going makeover. The present biographical picture of him rests upon far too many misconceptions and confusions with regard to his early years, and

---

have seen it in the library of the Faculty of Medicine in Lisbon (61–62).

25   Joaquim Veríssimo Serrão, *Itinerários de El-Rei D.Sebastião* (Lisbon, 1963), II, 49.

26   Of course there has been excellent work done on the institutional and political events of his reign, especially by Maria do Rosário de Sampaio Barata Cruz, *As Regências na Menoridade de D. Sebastão: Elementos para uma História Estrutural*, 2 vols. (Lisbon, 1983).

especially with regard to his sexual development. As Freud reminded us, and with reason, an individual's sexuality is the key, indeed the paradigm, for his character and personality and this was certainly as true of Sebastian as of anyone else. In Sebastian's case, his abnormal sexual development led to his remaining unmarried and without issue until his death without issue at age twenty-four, and it was these two factors that led directly to the Castilian "captivity" of the Portuguese Crown and state during the sixty years from 1580 until 1640.[27]

To better understand what happened to Sebastian, one needs to examine with attention the circumstances of his childhood. His father, an unfortunate victim of juvenile diabetes, died shortly (eighteen days) before his birth. Juana de Austria, his widowed mother and sister of Philip II of Spain, was a young foreigner without much if any support at the Portuguese court. In addition her marriage contract had specified that she would be free, if necessary, to return to Castile after doing her duty in producing an heir to the Portuguese throne. And return she did, some three months after his birth, not out of choice, or abandonment of her son, as some seem to think, but because she was ordered by her brother, Philip II, to replace him by acting as regent of Castile while he was away in England to wed Mary Tudor.[28]Thus, doubtless

---

27   The possibility of putting a Habsburg on the Portuguese throne if
      Sebastian had no issue was apparently already an idea of Charles
      V in 1557 when Sebastian was only three; see Marcel Batail-
      lon, *Études sur le Portugal au Temps de l'Humanisme* (Coimbra,
      1952), 267.

28   Those who accuse her of abandoning her son fail to understand
      the dynamics of royal family relationships in the sixteenth
      century, when female actions were still controlled by the wishes
      of the males. Women, for example, married whomever their male
      relatives chose for them; Philip II gave his daughters in marriage
      to the men of his choice. In the case of Juana, Charles V gave
      explicit instructions to his daughter about what she could and

with regret, but forced by circumstances, his mother left both
Portugal and her baby boy and returned to Castile, never to
lay eyes on him again, although she did write to him from time
to time, as well as sending emissaries to give her an account
of him. In addition she commissioned paintings of him to let
her see what he looked like.[29] As a result, Sebastian grew up
deprived both of a father who could act as his protector and
a mother in whom he might confide. In their stead respon-
sibility for his upbringing fell to his grandmother, Catarina,
wife of King João III, and his granduncle Henrique, João III's
brother. They in turn selected a set of caretakers for him,
the most important being an *aio* or guardian/foster father, D.
Aleixo de Meneses, and a tutor and a confessor. The choice
of the best persons to fill these posts was a matter of some
political conflict between his grandmother, Catarina, leader
of the Castilianophile group in the court, and his granduncle,
Cardinal Henrique, who headed the Portuguese "nationalist"
party. Catarina, who insisted upon Sebastian's sleeping in her
rooms at night until he was seven, and who made him take
his meals with her until late September of the year 1563,
when he was nine years old,[30] wanted either Frey Luís de

---

　　could not do regarding the minority of her son, including pre-
　　venting letters she sent to Portugal from being delivered and
　　making it clear to her that Spanish interests were paramount, and
　　her actions would have to conform to them. Thus she was obvi-
　　ously also obligated to put her brother Philip's wishes that she
　　return to Castile above any that she herself might have. Isabel D.
　　Braga, *Um Espaço*, 250–51.

29　Doubtless the painting by Christóvão de Morais of Sebastian
　　at age eleven now kept in the Convent of the Descalzas Reales
　　(Madrid) was one of these requested by his mother. See Annema-
　　rie Jordan, *Retrato de Corte em Portugal: O Legado de António
　　Moro* (Lisbon, 1994), 116–27.

30　*Relações de Pero de Alcáçova Carneiro*, Conde de Idanha, ed.
　　Ernesto de Campos de Andrada (Lisbon, 1937), 456. In 1566
　　Sebastian moved into his own quarters in the *Paço dos Estaus* (on
　　the north side of the *rossio*): Carneiro, 470. See also Damião de

Granada, a Dominican, or Frey Luís de Montoya, an Augustinian, for his tutor, while his granduncle Henrique insisted upon a Portuguese and a Jesuit. Cardinal Henrique's wishes prevailed and unfortunately, as it turned out, the role of tutor (and also that of confessor) was taken by Padre Luis Gonçalves da Câmara.

Câmara was one of the first generation of Portuguese Jesuits and came to court with a highly variegated past. He had been Ignatius de Loyola's amanuensis to whom he dictated his autobiography in 1553 and 1555.[31] He also had spent a considerable period of time in Muslim North Africa, where he was part of a group of Jesuits who undertook to give spiritual succor to Christian prison laborers in Tétuan. In order to "comfort" them as much as possible, his biographer says, Câmara and his colleagues took to sleeping alongside the prisoners in the dark semidungeons *(enxovas)*, where they were kept imprisoned when not working. It was during this period of service that Câmara reportedly became "ill" from an unspecified malady and went off to Ceuta to recover.[32] But more about the significance of all that later.

Thus, aside from his grandmother Catarina, the adult most constantly in contact with Sebastian was his tutor and confessor, Câmara. Aided by his assistant, Padre Amador Rebelo, who was entrusted with teaching Sebastian to read

---

Góis, *Descrição da Cidade de Lisboa*, trad. de José da Felicidade Alves (Horizonte, Lisbon, 1988), 53. There is also an English translation by Jeffrey S. Ruth, *Lisbon in the Renaissance* (New York, 1966).

31 John W. O'Malley, *The First Jesuits* (Cambridge, 1993), 8.

32 *"Cortavalhes o coraçam ver tantos Christaõs carregados de ferros, consumidos com o trabalho. **Pera mais os consolarem, se hiam dormir entre elles nas mesmas** enxovias* [bold emphasis mine] ... *Com os muitos trabalhos adoeceo o Padre Luis Gonçalves...":* António Franco, S. J., *Imagem da virtude em o noviciado da Companhia de Jesu na corte de Lisboa* (Coimbra, 1717), 27.

and write, Câmara undertook to instill in the child prince the rudiments of culture. Sebastian would sit in a chair indicative of his importance, while Câmara, facing him on a stool, would read the Latin and Portuguese texts the boy was expected to copy and absorb. The lesson period was carefully timed with an hourglass. In spite of those like Sebastian's grand-mother Catarina, who mistrusted him for reasons the sources never completely explain, Câmara was generally held in high repute due to the extent of his learning if not for the grace of his appearance. He was described as afflicted with a stammer ("*gago*") and looking ugly and "brutish" with one blind eye. His verbal discourse, however, was sweet and soothing and his manner suave and ingratiating.

And so matters went until Sebastian's ninth year (1564), when the boy first gave outward signs of a disturbing malady that was described as "seminal fluxes" or more specifically, a creamy discharge from his penis.[33] Doctors were called, plasters applied, bleedings done at night, etc., but good health never returned to Sebastian. Though physically strong and athletic, he thereafter suffered from numerous chronic physical complaints.

Given his importance as the guarantor, indeed the only assurance, of continued Portuguese independence and his significance on the European royal marriage market, there was considerable foreign interest in his personal medical problems. Phillip II of Spain, his uncle, went so far as to send special agents to the Portuguese court to keep him informed about the circumstances of Sebastian's health.[34] Even Cath-

---

33   It was described by Castilian agents at the Portuguese court as a "*cierta substancia ó purgacion*" that he expelled "*por sus organos.*" See Velloso, *Sebastião* (Barcelos), 54. See also footnote 22. The age when his discharges first began have been pushed back now to nine years.

34   Philip sent his agent Moura to check up on Sebastian in April of 1566 (Carneiro, 459); and Sebastian's mother again sent Moura to see her son in August of the same year "*por certa má disposição*

erine de Medici, given the potential of Sebastian as marriage material for a French princess, took note. And it was her agent at the Portuguese court, the baron of Fourquevaulx, who finally put his finger on the embarrassing truth about Sebastian's mysterious malady: without mincing words, he summed it up in a letter to her as "gonorrhea."[35]

How did Sebastian become infected? First we need to pay attention to his age when the malady first appeared. Today, and assuredly also in the sixteenth century, the appearance of a sexually transmitted disease in a nine-year-old boy is almost certain evidence of sexual abuse by an adult. And there is no reason to think that in the sixteenth century, the likely source would be far different from today—that is to say, almost always the culprit is found to be someone close to the child in whom he trusts and who exercises strong influence over him. In Sebastian's case, this would clearly be his tutor, Padre Luis Gonçalves da Câmara, who first became his confessor in 1560, a post that he held until 1566, the year after Sebastian's symptoms became known to the court, when he was dismissed by Sebastian's grandmother, Queen Catarina.

In contrast to most Portuguese historians, who are irritatingly vague about who was acting as Sebastian's confessor in 1563, when his disease first appeared, an eminent American specialist on the Portuguese Jesuits, Dauril Alden, is very clear on the matter. Câmara was made his tutor *and* confessor in 1560 but was replaced by Frey Luís de Montoya at the insistence of Sebastian's grandmother, Catarina, in 1566,

---

que teve dos rins" ("because of an illness he had in his kidneys"): Carneiro, 470. This undoubtedly refers to his penile discharges.

35 Velloso, *Sebastião*, 107: "…*une secrette maladie qu'on appelle gonorrée, à laquelle il est subject.*" Mário Saraiva's claim in *D. Sebastião: Na História E Na Lenda* (Lisbon?, 1994?), 58, that "wet dreams" or *espermatorriea* was called *"gonorreia"* at the time is preposterous. Although sixteenth-century physicians did not understand the etiology of gonorrhea, they definitely knew the difference between it and normal adolescent "wet dreams."

a year after the boy's sexually transmitted disease became court knowledge. (When Sebastian came of age to rule in his own right two years later, he reinstated Câmara as his confessor with the support of Cardinal Henrique.) [36] It seems quite possible that she had made some connection between Câmara and Sebastian's illness. An undated document published by Luciano Ribeiro tells of Catarina's dismay and frustration at her inability to alter Sebastian's "vicious" lifestyle.[37] Sebastian's guardian/foster father (*aio*), D. Aleixo de Meneses, also warned her that Câmara already knew the physical "nature" of the boy king and would soon take control of his mind.[38] The Portuguese word Meneses used for "nature" was "*natureza*," which carries a strong suggestion of his having a sexual "knowledge" of the king. One might note that the word "*natura*" was used by the Portuguese Inquisition at the time as a synonym for a male's genitalia.[39] In addition Montoya's eagerness to leave the position of confessor and relief when he did so would take on added meaning if he had been called in to replace a confessor with whom Sebastian had been having sexual relations.[40]

---

36   Dauril Alden, *The Making of an Enterprise: The Society of Jesus in Portugal, Its Empire, and Beyond, 1540–1750* (Stanford, 1996), 82.

37   Ribeiro, "Colectânea," 174–75.

38   Antero de Figueiredo, *D. Sebastião, Rei de Portugal* (Lisbon, 1924), 61. "*O padre* [Câmara] *já conheceu a natureza do rei; não tarda a apoderar-se-lhe do animo.*"

39   See António Borges Coelho, *Inquisição de Évora, 1533–1668* (Lisbon, 1987), 56. Further a Latin-Portuguese dictionary of 1570 defines *natura, ae* as *natureza* and *naturalia, ium* as "*Ho sexo do homem ou molher.*" Jerónimo Cardoso, *Dictionarium Latino-Lusitanicum & vice versa lusitanico latinum: cum adagiorum feré omnium iuxta seriem alphabeticam pertuilit expositione* (Coimbra, 1570), under "N."

40   Montoya is quoted as saying that the year he served as Sebastian's confessor seemed like "many centuries" to him and that he found the "air" of the palace "noxious" to holiness. Diogo

The possibility of sexual abuse in the confessional was great. The confessor-penitent relationship was ripe with temptations for unscrupulous and predatory confessors. In his study of sexuality in the confessional during the sixteenth and seventeenth centuries, Haliczer points out that

> As Freud was the first to acknowledge, power imbalance in a relationship can make for a potent aphrodisiac, and this was true of the confessional relationship. Kneeling before them during confession and revealing their deepest secrets, it became all too easy for penitents to idealize their confessors and for confessors to take advantage of their penitents' need for affection and approval.[41]

Even Jesuits were not immune to temptation, as a letter that Ignatius sent to members of the society seems to indicate. He advised them to make sure when they heard confessions from women *or young men* (italics ours) that they should have the penitent kneel beside their chair, not in front of it.[42]

Other fingers also point directly to Câmara as the source of infection. One piece of evidence indicates the high likelihood that Câmara himself was infected with chronic gonorrhea. Blindness in one (not both) eyes is a very common result of untreated gonorrhea, and as was noted earlier, Câmara was described as exactly that—blind in one eye.[43] Câmara also was ill through much of his adulthood, suffering from "many and great pains" that would certainly be consonant with

Barbosa Machado, *Memórias para a História del Rey D. Sebastião*, II (Lisbon, 1737), 616–19.

41 Stephen Haliczer, *Sexuality in the Confessional: A Sacrament Profaned* (New York, 1996), 109, 136–37, and passim.

42 O'Malley, *First Jesuits*, 148.

43 Velloso, "Histórica Política," in Peres, *História de Portugal*, V, 53: Câmara was "*muito feio, di brutta presenza, cego dum olho e gago.*"

chronic gonorrhea.[44] Additionally there is Camara's own statement in a letter to Rome in which he admits to knowing about
the king's illness a year before it became general knowledge
in court circles.[45] And finally there is the testimony of Sebastian's *aio* indicating concern about the relationship between
Câmara and Sebastian. In short Meneses was implying that
the confessor was already in control of Sebastian's body and
was intent upon gaining control over his mind too. In fact he
did just that, to such a degree that he became the object of a
furious attack upon himself and his brother, Martin, to whom
Sebastian in effect turned over the government of Portugal
upon reaching his majority in 1568. The attack came from
the eminent humanist Jerónimo Osório (1506–1580) in a
series of letters, his Cartas Portuguesas, that claimed Sebastian was being held "captive" by the two brothers Cãmara
and implied that their relationship with him was highly
"unsavory."[46] The idea that he was having sexual relations
with one or both of them also became common rumor when
anonymous fliers posted in public places in Coimbra accused
Sebastian of being *"abarregado"* (in a state of concubinage)
with the brothers.[47]

44 *"Mais* [Camara] *me disse, que tres cousas tinha pedido a Nosso
    Senhor, e eraõ huma doença comprida, padecer dores por seu
    amor, e morte com juizo perfeito, que as duas primeiras lhe tinha
    ja concedido porque auia muito estava doente e era afligido com
    muitas e grandes dores"*: Loureiro, *Relação*, 526.
45 See footnote 21.
46 Jerónimo Osório, *Cartas Portuguesas* (Coimbra, 1922). Admit-
    tedly some of Osório's anger could be attributed to the brothers
    Câmara having managed to replace him as advisors to the king:
    D. Jerónimo Osório, *Tratados da Nobreza Civil e Chistã*, trans.
    by A. Guimarães Pinto (Lisbon, 1996), 49–53. There are those
    who believe the author of the letters was not Osório but rather
    Pero d'Alcáçova Carneiro, but this does not affect the point that
    I make here.
47 J. V. Serrão, *História*, III, 65, fn. 192. *"Abarregado"* was a
    synomym for *"amancebado,"* or a relationship of concubinage:

The physical effects of Sebastian's chronic and incurable infection are clear from the sources. For example, he had pains in his groin or scrotum that shifted from left to right and that made it at times painful for him to ride horseback. He had characteristic eye inflammations. He slept fitfully, often getting up again after having gone to bed. And he suffered from fevers and chills ("*calafrios*") that he attempted to counter by wearing thick, warm leggings. All of these are typical symptoms of untreated gonorrhea.[48]

There were also psychological effects resulting from this trauma. First and most apparent was Sebastian's avoidance of women, so that he seemed almost allergic to them. As Faria y Sousa's *História del Reyno de Portugal* described the situation, "He had no desire for that which men desire most. The power of [feminine] beauty was banished from his eyes. There never was a woman whom he courted ... A young and handsome sovereign Prince detested his own nature and the marriage bed." [49]

Did Sebastian then simply abjure sex and sexual expression? Some pious historians apparently would like us to believe so. However, less naive people know perfectly well that young men seldom if ever renounce sex during the years when their libido is strongest, and while not every male victim of homosexual abuse becomes a homosexual himself,

see António de Moraes Silva, *Diccionário da Língua Portuguesa*, I (Rio de Janeiro, 1889), 54.

48   See *Merck Manual of Medical Information* (Whitehouse Station, NJ, 1997), 123. Taken all together, it is quite likely that his untreated gonorrhea resulted in Reiter's Syndrome, or "reactive arthritis."

49   Manuel de Faria y Sousa, *História del Reyno de Portugal ... en cinco partes ...* (Brussels; en casa de Francisco Foppens, 1730), 285: "*Desapetecia todo lo que mas apetecieron los hombres. Siempre à sus ojos quedò corrida la fuerça de la hermosura. Nunca uvo Dama que le diesse cuydado ... Un moço hermoso y Principe soberano aborrecia la propia naturaleza, y el talamo ...*"

that is certainly one possible outcome. Whether the person in question does or does not most likely depends upon environmental influences as well as a possible genetic disposition. In Sebastian's case, however, the evidence is clear that he did develop a homosexual orientation and apparently became a practicing one. Although his homosexuality is, of course, never explicitly stated as such in the sources, as far as I know, nonetheless it is clearly revealed in various stories (heretofore ignored as irrelevant or merely indicative of his odd behavior) about him and his activities during his youth and early manhood. For these we need to turn again to Manuel de Faria y Sousa's *História del Reyno de Portugal* and examine the accounts given there about Sebastian's unusual behavior. They present clear evidence that he often spent several hours at night searching about for homosexual opportunities or in what would be called "cruising" in present-day gay parlance.[50] A couple of passages from the *História* will make this clear: "Next to the Palace in Sintra there is a wood so thick that even during the day it is frightening to anyone who goes into it alone; but Sebastian often got up at night to go walking in it for a couple of hours by himself."[51]

The fact that this has either not been noticed or understood and certainly not discussed by Portuguese historians is most probably due either to their ignorance about or to their abhorrence and avoidance of what it suggests. Obviously Sebastian was not wandering in the woods lost in philosophical thought or contemplating the starry heavens. He was not the philosophical type and it would have been difficult, indeed impossible, to see the stars well, if at all, from under the trees in a thick woods. Rather it is likely—in fact I would say "certain"—that he was doing what young men who have no interest in women do when they ramble about in parks and

---

50   The Portuguese equivalent would be *"ir ao engate"* or *"passear a procura dum engate."*

51   Faria y Sousa, 286.

woods at night—seeking homosexual partners for quick sex.[52] But Sebastian's gay nighttime adventures did not always take place in the woods or forest near the palace in Sintra. At other times he met, apparently by some prearrangement, mystery men on the beach across the river Tagus or in the dunes behind the beach. Here is the passage describing such activities.

> After having gone to bed he got up again at around eleven at night with his pageboy[53] Don Álvaro de Meneses, and going out to the beach he went on ahead and after one or two hours came back. Often with Sancho de Tovar, at the same hour, he crossed the Tagus in a boat, jumped out onto the beach where he met another boat that had come from Belem from which another man emerged and after walking on the beach for one or two hours they went their separate ways without anyone knowing what he had been talking about or with whom.[54]

We cannot know how often he "scored" during his nighttime cruising expeditions since "normal" people who might witness what was happening were not out wandering in the woods or on the beach in the middle of the night. But his cruising for sex was apparently not limited to nighttime strolls in the woods around Sintra or on the banks of the Tagus River.

---

52   Indeed it is precisely for this reason that many parks in Paris (such as the Jardin de Luxemburg) are fenced and locked at night—to keep homosexuals out. In the late eighteenth century, Paris cruising took place in the wooded areas that occupy what is now the Champs Elysées: Jeffrey Merrick, 2002, "'Noctural Birds' in the Champs-Elysées; Police and Pederasty in Prerevolutionary Paris," *GLQ: A Journal of Lesbian and Gay Studies*, 8:3, 425–32.

53   On the homosexual relationships of young noblemen with their pages at the court of D. Sebastião, see footnote 62.

54   Faria y Sousa, *Historia*, 285–86.

There is also an account of an episode with a black boy in the woods near Almeirim that took place during the day and for which we do have witnesses. Here is the way the *História* tells the story:

> Another time in Almeirim he was waiting in a tree for a wild boar to pass by; when he sensed a rustling noise in the leaves he took a look and espied a bulky form; so he descended in a hurry and tackled it; the noise of the struggle brought some hunters to the place, thinking that the king was fighting with some monster, but they found him in the embrace of a savage black who days ago had run away from his master and was living with the wild beasts of that woods.[55]

The story needs to be recast, however, the better to reveal the actual sequence of events. It should be noted that the explanation for why he was found to be "embracing" a black man in the woods had to have come from Sebastian alone, since the puzzled hunter-witnesses only arrived after all this had supposedly taken place to find him already "in the black's embrace." Thus we can reconstruct the events as follows:

1. Some hunters in the woods near Almeirim heard loud noises that sounded like a struggle (*lucha*) and went to investigate.[56]

---

55   Faria y Sousa, *Historia*, 286: "*Otra* [*vez*] *en Almeirin sobre un àrbol esperava à un javali, sintiò ruido entre las ojas, e aplicando la vista distinguiò un bulto, baxò aprissa, e arremetiò con el: el ruido de la lucha hizo que acudiessen algunos caçadores pensando que el Rey lo avia con algum mostruo, y hallaronle abraçado con un negro salvage que de largos dias huido de sus amos habitava con las fieras de aquel monte.*"

56   It hardly needs to be pointed out that sexual intercourse, depend-

2. When they arrived they found young king Sebastian in the embrace of a fugitive black man.

3. Sebastian, surprised by their arrival, explained to them that he had been waiting in a treetop for a wild boar to pass by. When he heard a rustling noise in the leaves, he descended rapidly and attacked the figure, thinking it to be a wild boar, only to discover after struggling with it that it was a black fugitive slave.

His explanation must have puzzled his listeners, however. For one needs to remember that one did not go hunting for wild boar by oneself, not was it customary to wait for them in treetops and then jump down and attempt to wrestle them to the ground with one's bare hands, there being no mention of any weapon in the story. Rather they were hunted in an elaborately systemic manner by men on foot, assisted by *monteiros* and *moços*, along with a pack of attack dogs, and when the boar was cornered, it was killed with short daggers ("*azcumas*") or with spears.[57] Indeed, since the explanation given by Sebastian doesn't make much sense at all as reported, it is quite clear that what we have here, covered up, was a sexual liaison in the woods (that can, depending

---

ing upon intensity, can be noisy and sound like a person-to-person struggle.

57   See A. H. de Oliveira Marques, *Portugal na Crise dos Séculos XIV e XV* (Lisbon, 1987), 480: "*O* Livro da Montaria *foi um tratado completo da caça ao javali,* **utilizando a lança e matilha de cães**" (bold ours). See the *Livro de Montaria* in M. Lopes de Almeida, *Obras dos Príncipes de Avis* (Porto, 1981), 1–232. Indeed João I explicitly warns against trying to spy out wild boar by climbing trees: "*e outrosi lhes deue de defender que nenhum nom se suba a nenhua aruor ... ca seiam bem certos que qualquer que assi estiuer em aruor ... logo o porco passa, senom todauia que seiam em chaão*" (115). Also the edition of F. M. Esteves Pereira, *Livro da Montaria* (Coimbra, 1918), passim.

upon intensity, sound like a struggle or *lucha*) noisy enough to attract the attention of some nearby hunters who, when they arrived, found the young king in the arms of a black man. To explain the very odd circumstances in which he was found, Sebastian made up his implausible hunting story—a story strange enough to be remembered long after the event.[58]

The only reasonable interpretation of these odd stories is that Sebastian was engaged in nocturnal and sometimes daytime cruising expeditions, typical of homosexuals seeking anonymous sex. Given all the rest that we know about him, his allergic reaction to women, his preteenage gonorrhea, there can be really no other plausible explanation for a young king to be meeting strange men on the beach at midnight or be surprised in the woods in the embrace of a black man. More discreet sources merely refer to his spending his nights carousing with young men of ill repute,[59] but Faria y Sousa is much more explicit about what he or they were doing and make clear, I think, the homosexual nature of his nighttime forays.[60]

There is also further evidence that what affection he did feel and show was directed only to male friends. Another

---

58   It is also a very nice example of "transgressive sexuality."

59   Ribeiro, "Colectânea de Documentos," 176: "...*passeaua de noite cõ gente de pouca autoridade e menos mostras de uirtude.*"

60   It might be noted that the aforementioned biography by Villa-corta Baños-García finds in these same stories merely a "certain tendency or liking for the mysterious" on the part of Sebastian. His meetings with unknown men on the beach are transformed into the king's "listening with pleasure to the sound of the water or of the waves breaking at his feet" (86); his forays into the woods around Sintra are interpreted as "waiting for a wild boar to pass by (sic), [or] spending the night beneath the shelter of some tree ... while he filled himself with the odors and essences of nature (87)." Needless to say, none of these ingenuous explanations for his nocturnal forays are supported by the sources. Apparently even his Spanish biographer is too naive to divine the homosexual nature of the king's nighttime cruising.

passage in the *História* makes this clear: "Don Álvaro de Castro, his favorite, died and some nights Sebastian went out with some noblemen and leaving them some way behind went on the grave of Don Álvaro where they could hear him talking and then saw him come back with tears in his eyes."[61]

In addition, lest one think that homosexual activity would not have been tolerated at the court of King Sebastian, there is good evidence that, in spite of his own attempts to project a personal image of hypermasculinity through incessant jousting and hunting, the young noblemen of his court were not at all adverse to demonstrations of openly gay behavior, if we can credit a passage of Francisco Manuel de Melo in his *Carta de Guia de Casados*:

> ... and how can one believe that in the reign of King Sebastian, when men pretended to be made of iron in imitation of the excesses of the king, it was the custom for young noblemen to go around with their bodies pressed up against those of their pages, the way women do today. And this bad habit came to such a pass that when they played ball and went from one side of the court to the other they would not do so without calling their pages to come support them with their bodies. They would say "Haaaaa" stretching out the word and the rest of them spoke in an effeminate manner that was the custom of the time."[62]

---

61 Faria y Sousa, *História*, 286.

62 Francisco Manuel de Melo, *Carta de Guia de Casados* (1651), (Porto, 1963), 103–04: "...*como se poderá crer que naquele reinado de el-rei D. Sebastião, em que os homens se fingiam de ferro, por contemplação dos excessos de el-rei, era costume andarem os fidalgos mancebos encostados em seus pajens, como hoje as damas? E chegava a tanto aquele mau costume, que quando os que jogavam a péla, passavam de uma casa para outra, o não faziam sem que se lhes chegassem os pajens, e neles se encostassem. Diziam haã, fazendo-o muito comprido, e os mais*

If this was their behavior in public, what might not they be doing with their pages in private?

Let us therefore now sum up the arguments that we have presented regarding Sebastian's sexual abuse and the consequences of this for him and his reign.

1. There can be no reasonable doubt, given all the evidence, but that Sebastian contracted gonorrhea and/or chlamydia at age nine, and very possibly both since the two are often transmitted together. His "seminal fluxes" cannot be brushed away as nothing more than adolescent "wet dreams," since his "morbo" continued to recur, off and on, throughout the remainder of his life until his death at age twenty-four. Furthermore, since natural ejaculation normally begins in adolescent males around age twelve and a half, to have "discharges" as early as age nine is a certain indication of a sexually transmitted disease. Nor can it be argued that it was contracted "indirectly," as some pious historians have claimed, since this is virtually impossible in the case of sexually transmitted diseases.

2. Since the symptoms first appeared at age nine, it is virtually certain that he was infected as a result of some sexual initiation [today we would say sexual abuse]

---

falavam afeminado, por uso daquele tempo." The exact nature of the "*jogo da péla*" is uncertain, as well as the rules by which it was played. It involved a ball (*péla*), and may have resembled today's pelota or tennis. More investigation is needed. The term "*casa*" in the phrase "*passavam de uma casa para outra*" is defined in Morais e Silva, *Diccionário*, I, 420, as: "*no jogo da pella é a primeira divisão do topo do jogo e da o nome aos dois primeiros contendores.*"

by an adult. In virtually all cases—and this would be as true in the sixteenth century as in the twentieth—such abuse comes either from a family member or someone closely associated with the family who occupies a position of trust and has intimate contact with the youngster. In Sebastian's case, this would almost certainly be his tutor and confessor. His *aio* Meneses could hardly be the guilty party, for he was highly critical of the unhealthy relationship and dominant role that his confessor had over Sebastian. Furthermore, we do have two pieces of evidence that provide a means to identify the abuser.

a) The statement of Meneses that Câmara had already gotten to "know the nature of the king" and was next attempting to gain control of his mind. In the context, Meneses's use of the word *"naturaleza"* needs to be read in a physical sense, referring to the dichotomy of body vs. soul. In short he implied that Câmara had already gained carnal knowledge of the king and was next attempting to gain control of his mind.

b) Sebastian's confessor, Luis Gonçalves da Câmara, was blind in one eye, a common and visible symptom of untreated gonorrhea. Although one cannot know for certain where or how he became infected, it seems quite likely that this could have been while sleeping with the Christian captives in Tétuan.[63] Thus our conclusion that of the various people around Sebastian at the time it was most probably Câmara who had gonorrhea and therefore the most likely person

---

63   See footnote 32.

to have transmitted the disease to Sebastian, almost certainly during a private session of confession. It is also interesting to note that Sebastian, in contrast to even the most pious members of the court, appeared strangely attached to confessing very often, going every week instead of only once a year as was customary for most members of the court.[64]

3. Sebastian's various ailments as they are related by contemporary sources all are consonant with the diagnosis that he suffered from untreated gonorrhea. He had the penile discharges that are the primary symptom of gonorrhea. He also had pains in his scrotum that shifted from his left side to his right and back again, which are also typical of untreated gonorrhea, severe enough that he found it painful at times to mount to ride horseback. In fact, taken all together, one can say that his untreated gonorrhea may have produced Reiter's syndrome (reactive arthritis) in Sebastian. The only treatments that he is known to have received from his doctors were the application of *"emplastos"* and bleedings at night; the latter in turn were most likely the cause of the *"tonturas"* and fainting spells from which he suffered

---

64   Francisco de Sales de Mascarenhas Loureiro, "'Relação da vida d'ElRey D. Sebastião' do Padre Amador Rebelo," *Revista da Faculdade de Letras de Lisboa*, IV série, 1978:2, 508–09. Rebelo tells an amusing story about Sebastian, then age six and a half, asking an old hermit how often he confessed. The hermit was reluctant to answer but finally, Sebastian insisting, said he did so once every day. Sebastian then asked what he had to confess every day. At this the hermit became enraged and replied that one needs to repent one's sins every single day saying *"tibi soli peccavi"* three times in a loud voice. This left Sebastian so astonished that from then on he made sure to confess once each week.

since these would be logical result of the excessive
blood loss from repeated bleedings; later "syrup of
endive" intended to "cool" his liver was given him
by mouth.

4. Sebastian's personality also displayed a number of
the psychological symptoms that often result from
sexual abuse. He was disassociative, as his written
letters demonstrate; he took refuge in an obsessive
pursuit of hyper-masculine activities such as jousting
and hunting; and he demonstrated an affective
coldness that made him shun all feminine contact
and company as well as skillfully and persistently
avoid marriage. In addition his vivid imagination
centering upon the idea of leading a ill-conceived
crusade against Islam soon got out of control and took
possession of his mind, with the result that he finally
met his death on the battlefield of Alcácer Kebir.

Indeed, I would go further to suggest that the abuse he
suffered may well have created in Sebastian unconscious
wishes for suicide.[65] I would not see his determination to go
into battle against the sultan of Morocco from which he could

---

65 *Journal of the American Medical Association* (2001); 286: 3039–
    3040: "Adults who suffered abuse ... during their childhood are
    more likely than their peers to attempt suicide decades later." It
    might be noted that Sebastian earlier gave evidence of a possible
    unconscious death wish by choosing to engage in an act of
    reckless bravado. Faria y Sousa again supplies the story. Sebas-
    tian had ordered that no ship should pass beyond the Belém
    Tower or São João without being registered. If it did, it should
    be bombarded by artillery and sunk. In order to determine if his
    orders were being carried out—"*o por que buscava la muerte*"—
    he and some noblemen got into a bergantine and violated the
    regulation. They were duly fired upon but survived; Sebastian
    afterward went back to the palace without revealing that he had
    been among those in the bergantine: Faria y Sousa, *História*, 286.

not be deterred as nothing more than an inexplicably stupid obsession. From what we now know about the psychological consequences of child abuse, it would seem perfectly reasonable to detect a death wish in such a desire. Whether or not Sebastian had any *conscious* death wishes when he was as young as fifteen (and I believe he did not), it is undeniable that he was already fascinated by the subject of dead Portuguese kings. Fleeing Lisbon in 1569 because of the plague, he and his entourage travelled north, ostensibly to visit the monastery of Alcobaça. Upon reaching the monastery Sebastian suddenly was taken by what Queirós Velloso calls a "sick impulse" to see some of his ancestors face to face, as it were. He therefore ordered that their tombs and eternal resting places be pried open so that he might gaze upon their remains. Here is the story as recounted by Velloso:

> Around the end of May of 1569 the first signs of the plague began to appear in Lisbon...during the month of June the illness advanced so rapidly that there could no longer be any doubt about it; and on the 22nd of June the King left for Sintra...[then] To distance himself further from the capital, Dom Sebastião left for Óbidos [where he] stayed a few days. On the 22nd of July he proceeded to Alcobaça lodging in the monastery [there]. One day he had the sick impulse to order the tombs of his ancestors opened. No one dared to dissuade him. The first graves violated were those of the kings D. Afonso II and D. Afonso III; afterward, those of their respective consorts, the queens D. Urraca and D. Beatriz. The enormous body of D. Afonso III impressed him; and it merited words of praise from the king him for his having completed the conquest of the Algarve. The other ruler, always in conflict with women, never added even a foot [*palmo*] of land to the kingdom. The tomb of King Dom Pedro

could not be opened without doing irreparable damage to the delicate sculptural work that decorated it. Let it be, exclaimed Dom Sebastian; and he condemned with harsh words his feminine nature. These insults outraged one of the most illustrious members of the Order, Friar Francisco Machano, a doctor of the University of Paris, who dared to address the king, criticizing him for thus insulting his predecessors who although they did not conquer foreign kingdoms had known how to maintain and govern their own. Sebastian took this rebuke so ill that the cardinal [Sebastian's uncle Henry] and administrator and abbot of Alcobaça were obliged to rebuke the courageous monk.

The next year (1570) during the month of October, Sebastian decided to visit Coimbra.

Passing through Batalha [enroute to Coimbra] he ordered the grave of King D. João II to be opened. The cadaver was intact and the garments that covered him showed no signs of the 75 years that had passed since the burial. Sebastian looked at it in silence mixed with fear and admiration. Then he ordered that the corpse be stood upright, and he took the dead king's sword [with which he had been buried] in his hand. "This was the best occupant ever for the throne," proclaimed the king to those around him. And he told the Duke of Aveiro, D. Jorge de Lencastre, to kiss the hand of the corpse. "My King," he exclaimed when the cadaver was put back to rest in the tranquility of the tomb.[66]

His naïve Spanish biographer terms this strange behavior

---

66   Velloso, *Sebastião*, 126–30.

"necrophilia." This is patently absurd. There was no sexual stimulation involved, merely a morbid curiosity about death and reflections upon the bravery or lack of it in his ancestors. Still, in a very real sense, Alcácer Kebir was already adumbrated there in the dank cloisters of Alcobaça that day when Sebastian, perhaps for the first time, looked death in the face, and the unconscious roots of the idea of being or becoming a dead king planted themselves in his mind and began their lethal growth.

In short I would argue that Sebastian bit by bit came to sense, unconsciously, that his crusade in Africa would lead to his death (or if by some miracle it did not, then to a greater glory than he could otherwise ever have dreamed of acquiring), and it is precisely for that reason that he so relentlessly pursued it.

Needless to say, one can never know exactly the deepest recesses of the human heart. This is especially true of an historical figure such as Sebastian. But if he knew, as he must have known, that he could never fulfill his primary duty of producing an heir and that the pressure on him about this matter as well as the humiliation of being unable to satisfy it would only grow more intense as time went on, it is entirely conceivable that his unconscious drove him to seek to end it all in a blaze of military glory. Thus viewed, his quixotic obsession with a "crusade" in Africa would not be the product of an overzealous religiosity or the simpleminded recklessness that it has traditionally been painted to be, but rather a tormented young man's desperate and tragic option for a dramatic way out of the impossible situation in which he found himself; a fateful, albeit unconscious, decision to invite death in battle at the head of a Christian crusade.[67]

---

67   Cf. the remarks of Torquato de Sousa Soares, *Antecedentes da Crise de 1580* (Coimbra, 1962), 38, who suggests that Sebastian, aware that he was unable to produce an heir to the throne, deliberately sought his death in Africa. Soares was a conserva-

* * *

The time is now ripe, therefore, for a new look at the life of King Sebastian. A new biography of the king, celebrated in Western literature and myth for his tragic, pathetic and symbolic significance, is in order.[68] But what is most needed is not more accumulation of data about Portugal and its government and society at the time,[69] but rather a completely new look at the man himself, at his psyche,[70] and especially his sexuality. All extant biographies suffer from the long-standing confusion surrounding his health and his persona and his "irrational" obsession with the conquest of Morocco. None of them show any sympathetic understanding of him, a sexually abused boy who was left to deal with the consequences of his experience alone and without help. With the untreated gonorrhea and its long-term effects, the psychological wounds, and the relentless pressures upon him to become involved with women, to marry and produce heirs, as predicted by his horoscope, a crueler fate it would be difficult to imagine.

Indeed, with the insight of a great novelist, Evelyn

---

tive historian during the Salazarist period; that makes his ideas all the more surprising.

68   Sebastian's image in English literature is covered in Maria Leonor Machado de Sousa, coord., *D. Sebastião na Literatura Inglesa* (Lisbon, 1985) while Ana Maria Pinhão Ramalheira deals with his last battle in German literature: *Alcácer Quibir de D. Sebastião na Alemanha* (Coimbra, 2002).

69   This is not to minimize the excellent work done on the period by Joaquim Veríssimo Serrão and especially Maria do Rosário Barata Cruz.

70   Let us recall here J. V. Serrão's remark that any new biography will need to be more psychological than ... documental (see footnote 14). Indeed, a new biography of Sebastian, written by Professor Maria Augusta Lima Cruz of the Universidade do Minho (Braga, Portugal), was published in 2006, but does nothing to improve our understanding of Sebastian as a person. See following essay.

Waugh probably came closer to the truth about Sebastian than have any of his numerous historians. In infusing the story of King Sebastian, like a kind of background perfume, into his great novel, *Brideshead Revisited*, Waugh made *his* Sebastian, Sebastian Flyte, into a golden youth of no great intellect who never managed to emerge from adolescent homosexuality, and who was ultimately fated to end his days as a derelict beggar in Africa. Obviously the Sebastian of *Brideshead Revisited* differs in many respects from Sebastian the Portuguese king. But in the essential perception that homosexuality precluded him from living the "normal" life of marriage and children that was expected of him, as well as his final "solution" of flight to and exile in Africa, Waugh recapitulates the problem of King Sebastian perfectly.[71] Tragically infected with gonorrhea and introduced to homosexuality, almost certainly by his tutor-confessor, Sebastian the king, like Sebastian Flyte, led a tormented youth, taking refuge in an obsessive fixation on hypermasculine sports and finally, in an attempt to eradicate his demons, a hopeless battle in the sands of North Africa that he must have known, if only unconsciously, would bring the final resolution of his problems that he sought.

Consequently, instead of simply repeating facile criticisms of Sebastian's ability to rule, criticisms that are based on a gross misunderstanding of his situation, any new biographer must be capable of a true appreciation of his uniquely

---

71   Pressured by the councilmen (*edis*) of Lisbon with regard to the danger of going to war in Africa without leaving behind a heir in case of his death, Sebastian responded by saying that he was already married but could not say with whom. Such a statement would be inexplicably bizarre coming from an heterosexual king, but perfectly understandable from a homosexual who felt it necessary to lie when pushed into a corner about being single. Joaquim Veríssimo Serrão, "D. Sebastião à Luz dos seus Itinerários," *Actas do Colóquio O Sebastiamismo, Política, Doutrina e Mito* (secs. XVI-XIX) (Lisbon, 2004), 29.

tragic situation as well as possessing the empathy needed to understand a young man who can only, I submit, be seen as a tragic victim of sexual abuse with all its physical and psychological consequences.

Through a Glass Darkly

A Disappointing New Biography of
King Sebastian of Portugal

CIRCULO DE LEITORES has initiated a series of welcome biographies of Portuguese rulers. One of the first is that of Dom Sebastião by Maria Augusta Lima Cruz of the University of the Minho.[1] It is a solid workman (or workwoman)-like survey of the most recent research regarding his reign, the bulk of which merits little discussion or dissent. The parts dealing with the events, the economy, the institutional developments, the empire, and so on and so forth really require little or no comment.

It is quite otherwise, however, with her treatment of Sebastian, the man, his personality, and particularly his sexuality. More than with most Portuguese rulers his homosexuality and its causation are a key element to his reign since as a result he left no heirs. Consequently after his death in 1578 and the short reign of his moribund old granduncle, King Henry (1578-1580), a lifelong ecclesiastic also without progeny, Portugal fell into the hands of the Habsburg dynasty, thus beginning the Babylonian Captivity that lasted for sixty years, or two generations (1580-1640).

What is deeply distressing about her biography is the

---

1   Maria Augusta Lima Cruz, *D. Sebastião* (Lisbon, 2006).

fact that in regards to Sebastian, the man, the author has not been able to go much beyond the characterization of him that was put together during the period of the New State and that might well be termed the "fascist/reactionary" portrait of him. Indeed it is quite amazing the degree to which contemporary Portuguese historiography still clings to the image of him that was elaborated to accommodate the concerns of the fascist culture of the New State so dominated by the sexual hypocrisy and the taboos imposed by the religious establishment at the time.

Here it should be recalled that Queiroz Velloso, the great authority on Sebastian and author of the best biography of him to date, reached the conclusion almost 80 years ago[2] that Sebastian suffered from a sexually transmitted disease, most likely gonorrhea, contracted around age eleven[3] but that Velloso declined to investigate further, no doubt fearing that he was entering dangerous ground. He wiggled out of the cul-de-sac in which he found himself by maintaining that the disease must have been acquired "indirectly" and thus avoided any discussion of possible sexual abuse of a Portuguese king at an early age. Unfortunately Velloso's chapter appeared precisely when Salazar, a devoutly Catholic professor from Coimbra University, was putting the final touches on his New State and, instead of building on what Velloso had achieved, historians of royalist and reactionary persuasion lost no time in writing to deny and refute his conclusion.[4] We

---

2　Queiroz Velloso, "História Política," in Damião Peres, ed., *História de Portugal* (Barcelos, 1933), V: 53-59.

3　Both Cruz and I have pushed back the date at which Sebastian's malady appeared, Cruz maintaining that it first became evident when he was nine and a half (mid-1563). See Lima Cruz, *D. Sebastião*, 123.

4　Among them Joaquim de Moura Relvas (b. 1898), Mário Saraiva, noted member of the Catholic/fascist movement, Integralísmo Lusitano (b. 1910); and Joaquim Veríssimo Serrão (b. 1925), all persons agreeable to the Salazar regime.

were told that Sebastian's penile discharge(s) were merely "wet dreams" and nothing more. Or, if not "wet dreams", then a chronic urethritis. Historians with medical degrees (or claims to such) weighed in to tell us that gonorrhea at the time didn't mean what gonorrhea means today, etc. Other diagnoses of his "malady" soon appeared. He was epileptic, said some; others that he suffered from diabetes and so on and so forth.[5] Finally the matter became sufficiently confused so that Portuguese historiography could conclude that the topic was far too mysterious to understand and that we would have to leave it at that. In short nobody could know what Sebastian's illness was all about and therefore the truth could never be known. This was doubtless comforting for many. However even a few of those adhering to this view did venture to admit that "someday" a closer investigation of Sebastian's psychology just might open up a way to the truth about him and his mysterious illness.[6]

One might have hoped that Professor Cruz would have taken it upon herself to accomplish this task. But sadly enough all she has done is to argue in circles about the matter and end up with exactly the old fascist/reactionary idea that Sebastian's illness is still too "mysterious" to understand. What is ever sadder is that she had before her a closely reasoned essay that cleared away the confusions and went directly to the issue, concluding that Sebastian was sexually abused at age nine or ten, almost certainly by his confessor, Luis Gonçalves da Câmara, that he became infected with gonorrhea as a result, and that this tragic sickness dogged his short life to the very end. This work was my essay published in 2004.[7]

---

5   Joaquim V. Serrão, *História de Portugal* (Lisbon,1978), III: 69-70.

6   Serrão, ibid.

7   Harold B. Johnson, *Dois Estudos Polémicos* (Tucson, 2004), 45-83. Interestingly Interestingly enough I sent her a preliminary draft

Instead she chose to reject my thesis and stick to the time-honored fascist/reactionary interpretation. The arguments she employs fall generally into two categories. One is to simply ignore or downplay or distort a number of my arguments and the evidence I present when it suits her, not bothering to actually refute any of it but rather proceeding like a judge or jury that excludes much of the evidence before reaching its verdict. For example on pages 86-87 of her biography where, faithful to the fascist image of him, she tries to explain away the multiple testimonies I cite about his avoidance of women, recoiling even from their touch, provided by Padre Amador Rebelo and others, by calling them "pouco concludentes" (page 86). The most that she is willing to admit is that Sebastian had what she terms "serious difficulties" in his relationship to women[8], referring on page 10 to his "misogynistic" nature. Later on page 261 she claims not to know whether reports of his nighttime wanderings in the woods (homosexual "cruising") and elsewhere "have any foundation", although she admits that his behavior was "extravagant". This, she claims, has led "certain historians"

---

of my study and received in return from her a pleasant letter thanking me for it and saying that my interpretation had never occurred to her but that it would be helpful to her in writing her book. Somewhat afterward when I published my essay in book form that also included an exchange of letters between me and an eminent professor of the University of Coimbra in which I attack his arguments, I sent her a copy but this time never received any thanks or acknowledgement and never heard from her again. I have to suspect this was because she did not want to associate herself with someone whose letter had likely given offense to an important Coimbra professor, and also wished to avoid the professional danger of adopting a novel and "revolutionary" interpretation penned by a foreigner.

8   This dismissal of the testimony of Rebelo is typical of her meandering, often contradictory argumentation that tends to "muddy" issues. Elsewhere she had praised Rebelo as "testemunho singelo" (Lima Cruz, *D. Sebastião*, 10).

to create "extravagant fantasies" (apparently for her homosexual "cruising" is an "extravagant fantasy"). Indeed in an
attempt to underline the "extravagance" of the "fantasies"
she also dredges up rumors of heterosexual dalliances to
muddy and confuse the evidence about what were clearly his
homosexual nighttime adventures, apparently not realizing
that he would have no reason to pursue women in the woods
at night since unlike the pursuit of sex with men, that would
have been highly acceptable behavior about which he could
be completely open. Even the explicit statement of Juan
de Silva, Phillip II's ambassador to Portugal in 1578, that
Sebastian was "impotent" (i.e., homosexual) is passed over
as of little significance. (page 261). In short, it seems clear
that she has no awareness of male sexuality nor insight at all
into typical homosexual behavior, in other words, no "gaydar"
to use an American colloquialism, and wishes to sweep all
the evidence of it under the rug.

The second is her confusion or naiveté about gonorrhea
and sexually transmitted infections.[9] This is reflected in her
meandering and disorganized arguments that don't in any
way support her conclusion that he had no sexually transmitted disease. One suspects that here the cause may well be the
Portuguese atmosphere of homophobia in which she doubtless has grown up, including the a priori idea that no Portuguese king could possibly ever have been sexually abused
(least of all by his confessor) or developed into a homosexual
since such things simply don't happen to such exalted personages.[10]

---

9   See Johnson, *Dois Estudos Polémicos*, on all this (passim).

10   Here it might be useful to point out that if 5 to 10% of all males
     are homosexual, as experts have estimated, one could expect on
     a statistical basis at least two or three homosexual Portuguese
     kings. But for Portuguese historiography, these evidently have
     never existed and statistics do not apply. As for exalted persons
     not being homosexual we have the unpublished "devassa" of
     1591 concerning "casos de sodomia e molicie, muito vulgares

While Cruz sensibly rejects the claims made by some that gonorrhea in the 16th century did not mean what it does today, she refuses to credit the explicit statement of the French ambassador at Sebastian's court who identified Sebastian's ailment as such, never giving a reason for not doing so. First appearing in English in 1526, the word gonorrhea referred to an unusual discharge from the penis, distinct from mere spermatorrhea. Although it was often confused with syphilis it was never confused with common spermatorrhea. In fact Cruz herself admits that the discharge began when Sebastian was nine and a half years old, and thus it could not possibly have been spermatorrhea. Nevertheless, ignoring the import of that fact, she goes on for several paragraphs discussing this "possibility" that she could and should have discarded at once.[11] Then while finally admitting that the claim that the discharge was mere spermatorrhea is untenable, she still refuses to accept that it was a sexually transmitted disease. Instead she takes refuge in the idea that it was a "chronic" urethritis. She cites a report that Sebastian expelled "unas arenas" in 1563 to suggest that this may have been the cause,

---

então em Lisboa mesmo entre pessoas da mais alta qualidade..."
(Biblioteca Geral da Universidade de Coimbra, MS. 535, fl. 131).

11   Indeed at the end of her discussion of his illness she goes on to cite some passages from Leviticus to conclude that Sebastian's discharge was regarded at the time as something other than mere spermatorrhea (Lima Cruz, *D. Sebastião*, 124-125). She also seems not to have noticed that in 1630 it was thought that Portuguese boys were too young to produce semen at age twelve (see Johnson, *Dois Estudos Polémicos*, 57, fn. 109). If they were not doing so at age twelve in the 17th century it is virtually impossible that they were doing so earlier in the sixteenth century. Additionally, as Buescu reports, the royal court was surprised that Sebastian's father, João, was able to have children at age 14 in spite of being "very young". Thus at the time fourteen years of age was evidently regarded as unusually early for a male to produce sperm. See Ana Isabel Buescu, *Catarina de Áustria, Infanta de Tordesillas, Rainha de Portugal* (Lisbon, 2007), 290.

adding her opinion that "any interpretations that go beyond a non-gonoccocal cause seem abusive." (page 124). To support this position she cites (via Alfonso Danvila) a long dead (and medically outdated, one might add) American doctor, one Frank Hughes, who opined that urethritis might have been the explanation.[12] And what really lies behind this idea? The "conviction" that Sebastian was always "chaste" and thus evidently could never have had sexual relations with anyone! Here her naiveté becomes crystal clear. Evidently she believes that the sexual contact that Sebastian could easily have had with his confessor when closeted with him would promptly have been made known to everyone. And since Sebastian or Câmara never told the world about it, [13] then it could not have happened. The fact that Sebastian's grand-mother, Catarina de Austria, developed an intense hatred of Câmara, well documented in the recent biography of Ana Isabel Buescu[14] and used by me to argue that the cause might very possibly have been intimations she received of sexual activity between Sebastian and his confessor, she dismisses,

---

12   The passing of small kidney stones is highly unlikely to produce chronic urethritis. Rather the latter is almost always the result of a bacterial infection. Since Sebastian's malady continued to the end of his life, her choice of this explanation lacks any convic-tion to medically informed people.

13   It should hardly be necessary to point out how common was sexual activity (whether hetero or homo) in the confessional. The Inquisition records are full of such evidence. See Stephen Haliczer, *Sexuality in the Confessional: A Sacrament Profaned* (New York: Oxford University Press, 1996). Câmara, his confes-sor, it should not be forgotten, suffered from a typical result of untreated gonorrhea: blindness in one eye, something Cruz com-pletely ignores. See Johnson, *Dois Estudos Polémicos*, 69.

14   Ana Isabel Buescu, *Catarina de Austria*, 376-379. Cruz fails to give sufficient attention to the significance of these events described by Buescu who suggests that knowledge of Câmara's abuse of Sebastian might be one of the causes for Catarina's intense hatred of Câmara.

very conveniently, as coming only from a probably "apocryphal" source.[15] Another indication of her inability to put two and two together to get the "big picture" relates to Câmara's illness. Of his chronic illnesses, Cruz says, the worst was a probable "oftalmia" that he contracted in Tétuan. But what Câmara contracted in Tétuan, most likely, was gonorrhea that led to his notorious blindness in one eye, blindness in only one eye being a classic symptom of untreated gonorrhea.[16]

In sum, she seems oblivious to the clear medical evidence in the sources. Sebastian's seminal "fluxes" began before they could possibly have been due to adolescent "wet dreams". The idea that they resulted from some mysterious irritations of a temporary nature (such as tiny kidney stones that he apparently passed without difficulty) is also impossible since they continued throughout his life. That they were accompanied by numerous other effects typical of chronic gonorrhea she simply ignores. [17]

She seems unfazed by the fact that the French ambassador, an educated man of his time, explicitly states that Sebastian's malady is gonorrhea. Thus, by simply picking and choosing bits and pieces from all the evidence that I present, ignoring whatever does not fit her arguments, her rambling and disorganized discussion reaches what is probably a pre-

---

15   Cruz seems most troubled by the statement attributed to Meneses who told Catarina that Câmara already knew the "nature" of the king. Whether the source here is Meneses or José Pereira Baião is irrelevant to the validity of the evidence. Indeed she herself is happy to use Baião as a source when it suits her, as on pages 95 and 96 of her book. That Frei Luís de Montoya, who served as Sebastian's confessor for a year or two after Câmara was dismissed, claimed he found the palace atmosphere "moralmente nocivo" (see Johnson, *Dois Estudos Polémicos*, 68, note 130), she passes over as apochryphal (Lima Cruz, *D. Sebastião*, 126).

16   Cruz, *D. Sebastião*, 82. See Johnson, *Dois Estudos Polémicos*, 64-65.

17   See Johnson, *Dois Estudos Polémicos*, 70.

determined conclusion---to the extent that she reaches a conclusion---by agreeing with the old reactionary/fascist idea of Montalvão Machado that his illness was (and is) far "too mysterious" to understand. [18]

This is sad. Instead, I would argue that a modern Portugal, by now liberated from the traditional interpretations that were elaborated under the censorious watch of the fascist New State and the church to which it deferred, at last deserves a modern biography of Sebastian that breaks through the old taboos and has the courage to get to the truth. Since Sebastian was among the few Portuguese rulers who were homosexual, one would have hoped that Cruz would not only have admitted the fact but indeed would have emphasized it, to make clear that Portugal has put behind it and escaped from the homopho-bic ecclesiastical mentality that dominated the Estado Novo. Unhappily this biography does not do that. Rather as far as Sebastian the man is concerned, it ends up as a neoreaction-ary account of his life that endeavors to keep his "illness" in the traditional state of confusion and Sebastian's sexuality in the closet where he has been imprisoned for almost eighty years (1933-2010). We need something better and a biogra-pher with a more modern understanding of sexuality.

---

18   Lima Cruz, *D. Sebastião*, 124. Confusing a taboo topic by muddying the waters so that one can avoid an unwanted solution and ultimately conclude that it is all too complex to understand seems to be a popular technique in Portugal. Here one thinks of the Casa Pia case about the decades of systematic sexual abuse of male youths at the national orphanage where the evidence has been deliberately "muddied" to such a degree that the case has dragged confusedly through the courts for nearly six years, finally reaching a conclusion only recently.

Retratos Ignorados de D. Sebastião[1]

A Critical Review

QUITE RECENTLY (2008) a valuable, but also lamentably confused, little book was published in Portugal with the title Retratos Ignorados de D. Sebastião.[2] The intent was to reproduce, publicize and comment on some oil paintings of King Sebastian (1554-1578) that are seldom seen, as well as those of some other people connected to him. The book is unusually valuable because of the paintings that it reproduces, but confused since the author appears unable to understand what the most important painting in it tells us.

This painting, presently in the Uffizi Gallery in Florence, appears on the front cover of the book and will be the focus of this review. It portrays a grown-up Sebastian, probably around 1577 when he was in his early twenties, clearly identifiable from the customary reddish brown hair and the blue-gray eyes of his family, but astonishingly enough it also presents him with his face or complexion as it actually was ("warts and all") and not "improved" by the painter in order to remove various blemishes.[3] Thus what we see here, but in no other known portrait of

---

1 Bernardo da Gama Lobo Xavier, *Retratos Ignorados de D. Sebastião* (Estoril: Princípia, 2008).

2 Xavier, *Retratos Ignorados*.

3 Or, as was said at the time, "tirado ao natural," meaning without any alteration of his appearance.

him, is a sizeable red blotch on his right cheek as well as other skin eruptions on his face that confirm and are completely consistent with the epidermal symptoms of untreated gonorrhea. Indeed, the pinkish red blotch is exactly the same as that seen in clinical pictures of victims of that disease.

The author however adamantly refuses to understand what the portrait clearly shows. Instead he soon launches into effusive about Sebastian so extreme that it would surely have embarrassed even the most extravagant worshippers of the king, such as the historian Carlos Malheiro Dias.[4] For instance, in Chapter V, pages 75–81 (entitled "Rendição e

---

4　　Maria Mota, "Sob o Signo de Prometeu: A polémica Sebastianista entre António Sérgio e Carlos Malheiro Dias (1924-1925)," to be found on the internet at http://conferencias.ulusofona.pt/index. php/lusocom/8lusocom09/paper/viewFile/162/138. Here is a part of the article:

Para Malheiro Dias, na linha da geração de 90, ser português significava manter-se fiel a o património cultural tradicional. Para a ideologia nacionalista que enformava esta geração, ofendida nos seus brios nacionais pelo Ultimato, D. Sebastião era um herói nacional, como se pode verificar em muitos dos textos literários da época e, muito em especial no poema "O Desejado" de António Nobre, que exerceu enorme influência na poesia portuguesa deste período.

Politicamente, Carlos Malheiro Dias era um defensor do integralismo lusitano: a visão do mundo que enformava a sua defesa do culto sebástico era tradicionalista, monárquica e católica. António Sérgio, pelo contrário, era um espírito cosmopolita e democrata. Patriota, o seu patriotismo nunca se confundiu com o dogmatismo nacionalista, professado pelos monárquicos conservadores. Muito pelo contrário, a cidadania nacional fazia parte da sua representação como cidadão do mundo. Não por acaso era um "estrangeirado," termo que adjectiva aqueles que como ele defendiam a reintegração de Portugal no âmbito cultural europeu, o que exigia, na sua opinião, uma radical reforma das mentalidades, ou seja, a passagem de uma mentalidade dogmática e acrítica para uma mentalidade crítica e científica. Discordando da concepção patrimonial e memorialística dos defensores do tradicionalismo, as "pedras vivas" eram para ele,

Honra"), the author tells us of his "atraimento" (to Sebastian), and his "profundo asco" at the prevailing "visão depressiva" of the king. He goes on to denounce those who see Sebastian as "apenas um doente" when in fact, he avers, the king demonstrated "comprovada robustez e destreza" and "incontestável coragem, bravura militar e desprezo pela vida." Next comes an extended panegyric to this "gloriosíssimo Rei de Portugal" while also attacking the "assassinato moral de D. Sebastião" who was, he says, "um rei religiosíssimo, puro como Gaalez" even when under the influence of his confessor and teacher, Padre Luis Gonçalves da Câmara, "cuja virtude pessoal era incontroversa."[5]

Truth to tell, most of this is more than questionable. While there can be no doubt that Sebastian attempted, as do many homosexuals, to appear hyper masculine by incessantly jousting and horse riding, he was in reality reckless and foolish rather than brave, traits of character that cost him his life at the age of twenty-four. Likewise his outward religiosity was not unusual at the time for high born personages with little diversion in life other than to attend mass, perform religious rituals, and visit ecclesiastical institutions. As far as being as pure as "Gaalaz", he was allergic to women and thus may have appeared at the time as "pure,"[6] but in fact it is quite clear that he often cruised for sex with men at night and occasionally during the day.[7]

---

verdadeiramente, a Pátria, os homens vivos do presente e não o património herdado.

5   The author is, from what I can determine, presently a Professor of Law in the Catholic University of Portugal (Lisbon). The bulk of his education in the law came during the Salazar period according to his CV.

6   A Google search of the Internet failed to identify who "Gaalez" might be. One presumes the author is thinking of some morally pure figure of legend, most likely Galahad.

7   See Harold B. Johnson, *Dois Estudos Polémicos* (Tucson: Fenestra, 2004), 45-83.

Still the author admits to being troubled by the skin eruptions on Sebastian's face in the painting, so he offers readers a "retouched" and "improved" version that removes the blotch and eruptions, in a rather pathetic but amusing attempt to wish away their existence. Still there can be no doubt that he was aware of the facts about Sebastian's sexual disease since he quotes extensively from the recent biography by Maria Augusta Lima Cruz[8] where the issue is discussed at length; he refers to her work constantly. Yet, in spite of this he ignores the issue and refuses to acknowledge the facts that stare him in the face. Instead he gingerly admits that there might be some kind of malady evidenced by the painting, but opts finally for the evasive, "easy-out" explanation of "erysipelas" to explain the blotch and lesions.

But this diagnosis is impossible for at least three reasons. First, the skin lesions on Sebastian's cheek do not look in the least like erysipelas. Erysipelas lesions are caused by a bacterial inflection that disappears with time. They do not continue for years on end as did Sebastian's malady. Second, he obviously got this diagnosis from the biography written by Lima Cruz who misrepresents the evidence. She refers to Sebastian's letter to Philip II that he wrote on 19 July 1577, saying he had an illness in his eye, and then claims Philip's ambassador to Portugal said this was erysipelas. But he did no such thing. Earlier (10 July 1577) the poet/warrior Francisco de Aldana (not the Castilian ambassador Juan de Silva) wrote to Philip II's secretary, Gabriel de Cayas, saying that Sebastian had been indisposed by a "resipola" without indicating where it was on his body and adding that he was already much better. What Sebastian complained about in his letter to Phillip nine days later was not erysipelas but rather an ailment in his eye, in other words "pink eye" or gonococcal conjunctivitis characteristic of untreated gonorrhea

---

8   Maria Augusta Lima Cruz, *D. Sebastião* (Lisbon, 2006).

and not erysipelas.[9] Finally, the author himself undermines his own diagnosis by going on to say that it is unlikely the painter would have painted Sebastian with only a temporary skin eruption, erysipelas of course being a temporary skin eruption.[10]

In short, the portrait presented (1) gives clear evidence that the skin on Sebastian's face showed symptoms of untreated, chronic gonorrhea and (2) the author, like many Portuguese historians, evades the issue by using a "red herring" to explain away the skin lesions, but then contradicts his own idea by admitting that a painter would have been unlikely to paint temporary lesions. In presenting this confused farrago the author simply joins the main current of Portuguese historiography that refuses to admit that a Portuguese king could suffer from a sexually transmitted disease (STD) as do "ordinary" people.

Here is what we now know for certain. (1) Sebastian was infected at age nine with gonorrhea for which there was no

---

9 Joaquim V. Serrão, *Itinerários de El-Rei D. Sebastião* (1568-1578) (Lisbon, 1987), 427: "... a minha yndesposiçaõ dos olhos...". The letter of Francisco de Aldana of 10 July 1577 mentioning the "resipola" is published by Alfonso Danvila, *Don Cristobal de Moura, Primer Marques de Castel Rodrigo (1538-1613)* (Madrid, 1900), 858. Danvila dates the letter correctly on page 274 of his book, but gets things very confused on page 858 where he gives the year as 1587 instead of 1577 and the date as 10 June instead of 10 July. The correct dates can be deduced from the content of the letter itself where Aldana says he left for Portugal on Wednesday, 26 June, and arrived there on Sunday, 30 June. The Julian calendar is used and only these days of the week fit the dates mentioned. Cruz clearly conflates (either intentionally or carelessly) the "resipola" mentioned in the Aldana letter of 10 July with the pink eye Sebastian speaks of in his letter to Phillip II on 19 July 1577.

10 Xavier, *Retratos Ignorados*, 17, n.25: "Contudo, não se pode deixar de pensar que não é nada natural que um pintor de corte representasse o rei com uma feia mancha passageira ..."

effective cure at the time. There can be no doubt about the age or the malady (a discharge of pus from his penis). Such penile discharges at that age can only be due to a sexual infection. To attempt to present this as the result of irritation of the urinary tract is impossible since it continued throughout his life. (2) Everything else depends upon this fact. Almost all his subsequent symptoms are what would be expected in someone suffering from chronic gonorrhea. (3) And now we have the final visual confirmation of this in the oil painting of him that the author of this book recently "rediscovered" in the Uffizi Gallery where the king's face exhibits the dermatological effects of chronic gonorrhea.

Nevertheless,we should not be surprised by the persistent denial about Sebastian and his illness in Portuguese historiography. This needs to be viewed in the context of another persistent denial that went on for years in Portuguese society about the systematic sexual abuse of young boys at the national orphanage (the Casa Pia scandal). Many people of importance knew about this abuse (and indeed it was brought to the attention of the President of the Republic) but the response was simply to ignore it all and sweep it under the rug. In short the Portuguese elite simply refused to see "the elephant in the room" when it involved something "not nice" or "unpleasant", particularly of a sexual nature. However, when the Casa Pia scandal finally burst out into the open because of a courageous newspaper report impossible to ignore, Portuguese society was "overturned" with agitation and distress about the scandal. Little else was discussed for months. But when the time came to do justice in the matter, forces conspired to muddy the water and delay resolution so that it took from five to more than seven years (depending upon how one counts) for the trial to come to a verdict, now being appealed. In spite of the attempts to look the other way, it was crystal clear that for years the ongoing abuse had been ignored or covered up by systematic denial by those concerned.[11] Hence it should be no surprise that Portuguese historiography has likewise engaged in a similar denial about the sexually transmitted disease of King Sebastian. Denial with regard to homosexual abuse, both contemporary and historical, appears to be deeply ingrained in Portuguese society and the Portuguese mentality.

Still, one has to wonder for how long Portuguese historians can continue to ignore the facts about Sebastian and his malady. How long can they persist in running away from the truth about Sebastian's medical condition? In short, in the face of mounting and now the conclusive evidence presented by the oil painting reproduced in this book, namely that the young king suffered from chronic, untreated gonorrhea, what can possibly justify the contumacious denial of the facts, first elaborated by the reactionary fascist historians of the Salazar period, and that still prevails in important sectors of Portuguese historiography, including, sadly enough, the author of this work?[12]

---

11   http://en.wikipedia.org/wiki/Casa_Pia_child_sexual_abuse_scandal.

12   The outlook of the author is clear from his final words at the close of the main text: "FINIS LAUS DEO VIRGINIQUE MARIAE" (Xavier, *Retratos Ignorados*, 41) and the last words on the very last page of the book ("FINIS LAUS DEO") (Xavier, *Retratos Ignorados*, 88). On the genesis and rise of the reactionary/fascist interpretation of Sebastian, already foreshadowed by Malheiro Dias, see Harold B. Johnson, "Through a Glass Darkly; A Disappointing New Biography of King Sebastian of Portugal (A Review Essay)", *Portuguese Studies Review* 18 (2) (2011), 163.

www.ingramcontent.com/pod-product-compliance
Lightning Source LLC
Chambersburg PA
CBHW050408290526
45786CB00003B/1172